I Was Trained To Be A Spy

A True Story

By *Helias Doundoulakis*

Cover by Manny Halkas

I Was Trained To Be A Spy

A True Life Story

Helias Doundoulakis

To order additional copies of this book, contact:
Xlibris Corporation
1-888-795-4274
www.Xlibris.com
Orders@Xlibris.com
38690

Dedication

My life has exceeded many expectations. The success I have enjoyed as an American citizen is a direct result of my experience during the war and it is only fitting to dedicate this book to the two most influential people in my life. The first person was my brother, George, whose strong influence and connections made my escape to Egypt and enlistment into the OSS a reality. His postwar professional contacts enabled me to achieve unexpected professional glories. Sadly, he passed away this March.

I would also like to dedicate this book to my wife, Rita. Her support and companionship has always created for us a wonderful home over the years, and I am in her debt.

Table of Contents

Prologue

I am the son of the author of this book, and as I remember the summer of '69, about to turn fifteen and to become a man, I was to embark on a three month trip to the land of my ancestors.

With ample time to visit relatives, spread like a diaspora through the Balkan Peninsula and islands, I was to stay a little here and a little there, hopping from relatives in northern Greece to Crete. However, when I looked at my itinerary, I noticed that for two of those three months I would be the guest of a family I knew little about, a name I had only heard in passing conversations, and whose children were slightly older than me, but whose father was a spy, like my father, during the war.

"Are they at least distant cousins, once or twice removed?" I asked my Dad. "Who is this Mr. Yiapitzoglou anyway?", and "why can't I stay with relatives?" I asked. He tenderly answered, "He is better than relatives, and besides, you'll be taken all over Athens, to museums, beaches, and wherever else Mr. Yiapitzoglou's sons wish to take you." As I found out, Mr. Yiapitzoglou was a Greek Naval officer who together with my father, a corporal in the US army and a member of the OSS's SI sector, were sent on a difficult and treacherous assignment, lasting nine months, to Salonica, Greece's second largest city, during the German occupation of 1944.

The Yiapitzoglou name would occasionally surface during conversations at family get-togethers on Long Island, or at times when I'd hear my mother shout, "Cosmas Yiapitzoglou is on the phone from Athens!", at which time my father would drop whatever he was doing to speak to his beloved and long-time friend.

Prior to my departure, I began to have second thoughts of going, however. All this talk of "You'll love them", and "you'll be like family", began to make this trip out to be an obligation, and I was about to call it off.

Then, quite by accident while rummaging through my father's desk, I came upon an old, red "Prince Albert's Cigars" tin, in which I found a dozen or so worn, multi-colored ribbons with stars, and medals. They were my father's, from the war. But most interesting of all, at the bottom and almost unnoticed, was a small collar-button sized red pin, emblazoned with gold letters "OSS", in cloisonné style. When I asked my Dad about this pin, and why it was so small, he said that he wore it on his army jacket, that the smaller the medal, the more important it was, and that I would not be here today if it wasn't for a whole lot of luck and fate. He then added, "Mr. Yiapitzoglou was a part of my life during the war, and since he is (twenty years) older, he looked after me like a son. He will do the same for you."

With that, I felt a renewed enthusiasm for the trip, and left for Greece. True to my Dad's words, the Yiapitzoglou family took me in like one of their own. Over afternoon meals, Mr. Yiapitzoglou would recall the harrowing events between my Dad and him and the Gestapo, all the while filling my glass with cold beer. He couldn't get over the close calls they had, and how they never got caught. I'll never forget how we laughed when he told us about the accordion my father bought to play along with the neighborhood sirens, and the annoyed husbands who quickly complained, including the jealous and recently widowed landlady.

You may have read many fictional accounts of spies, in which the main character undergoes a metamorphosis, and by using his skills and ingenuity, survives another day, where it seems that the villain has bad aim, and is less smart than the hero. However, in this book, you'll find real people in real situations. You'll meet characters with their pain and misfortune, and the wit and courage of those who survived. You will read detailed descriptions of my father's peculiar spy training by the OSS and the British Intelligence Service. The reader will witness how a simple, un-assuming youth adapted to each spine-tingling situation, while working under the noses of the Gestapo, and the skillful ways he utilized to avoid capture. From his escape to Egypt, to his training at the OSS academy in Cairo, and to his final discharge from the army the reader will be held captive. *I Was Trained to Be a Spy* is sure to entertain both young and old, and for anyone who enjoys adventure, this book will not disappoint, and is a must reading for all who cherish the world of espionage.

Stephen Doundoulakis
August, 2007

Self portrait 1945

Chapter 1

- Introduction into the group of the OSS training spy school Cairo Egypt, October 1943

It was the first day, a mostly hot day in October 1943. An introduction to this peculiar form of war, "spy" training, if you will, in the Secret Intelligence and Special Operations section of the OSS outside Cairo, Egypt. A tall white-haired man with strong, piercing eyes walked in and, though we were sitting, commanded our attention.

"Good morning, gentlemen. I am Major Vassos, head of the training school for the Secret Intelligence section of the OSS. You are the chosen group, fifteen of you, ready to start training to become spies. And now let me ask any one of you, ahh . . . let me ask this gentleman in the front . . . what is your name?" And he turned to me, his eyes fixed on mine. I paused, and he continued in a stern monotone, "And remember, while you are here, you have no last name and will not use it."

"I am Corporal Helias D., sir," I said, rather unsure as to whether the use of the abbreviation was correct, and by his wide stare, I knew it was not.

"Tell me, Corporal Helias, is it day or night outside?"

I quickly responded, hoping to correct my error, "It must be day, sir, six o'clock in the afternoon, and it will be dark soon."

He again looked at me disapprovingly. "Gentlemen, as you can see, the corporal is not really sure if it is day or night! Well, after you finish training, I can assure you that you will convince anyone, even *me* that it is nighttime even though the sun is still shining! Your minds will be capable of fabricating imaginary realities or arguments that will convince anyone that whatever you are saying is true, friend or foe. Your training will last five months and will depend mostly on your ability to absorb what we will be teaching you and your ability to demonstrate to the teaching staff that you will be ready to undertake that important and dangerous mission. Not anyone can become a spy, but since you are here, it has been proved that you would be capable of undertaking dangerous missions."

He continued, "The instructions will be given by either OSS teaching staff or by members of English Intelligence Service. They've been around longer, so much the better for us. And their organization possesses more experience in certain things, which I'm not at liberty to discuss right now with you men."

Major Vassos, as I found out, was named John; and though he was tough, I liked him from the start. He had that impressive look as if he was, sometime in the past, a spy himself.

He said the training would be divided into eight classifications and enumerated for us the following:

1. Parachute jumping from various heights
2. Morse code and wireless instruction and operation
3. Commando training (defensive type)
4. Environment assimilation
5. Techniques in opening locks and safes for the purpose of photographing or stealing documents
6. Story fabrication and lying
7. Methods of escaping if captured
8. Elimination (how to kill in order to escape, if captured)

Afterward, Major Vassos introduced his group of instructors, all of whom were officers, and described the specialty of each instructor.

Besides the officers and instructors, there were many other soldiers in the compound, all with at least a sergeant's rank assigned in various other tasks. In addition, there were over twenty more helpers, cooks, cleaning personnel, and others.

While the major spoke, I stood as if I was hypnotized and asked myself, was it really me they were calling? Had I really been chosen to be part of this, a young man with a simple background, who had just come only a short time ago from a little village of Crete? And to find myself now a corporal in the U.S. army and a member of the OSS and ready to be trained to become a spy?

What I wasn't thinking about was that I was carefully chosen by the OSS, not randomly taken, considering my past two years in the Cretan resistance under the English Intelligence Service; the fact that I spoke English, Greek, and a little German; and the fact that I was born in the USA and was also an American citizen. I was to become an agent of the OSS, a spy, and an integral part of the American spy network in Greece. While the major dismissed us, I sat, finally grasping the reality.

For the reader to be able to follow step-by-step my advancement from being a small-town boy to becoming a prospective spy, I will have to go back to the time when I was in high school in Heraklion, Crete, in 1941.

Chapter 2

- Battle of Crete
- Joining Cretan resistance
- Escape From Crete to Egypt on a British torpedo boat

To show how the writer was chosen to qualify as a prospective spy, the writer is going back to a time when he and his brother, George, were members of the English spy network in Crete, from 1941 to 1943. There will be a description of the escape of a group of fifteen people to the south shores of the island of Crete as they tried to avoid capture by the German Gestapo. And the evacuation by an English torpedo boat from Crete to North Africa and eventually the trip to Cairo, Egypt, in June 1943, will follow.

By April 1941, German troops had occupied most of Greece. Some of the Greek isles were not under Nazi control. One of these islands of strategic importance was Crete, the largest of the Greek islands and situated between mainland Europe and Libya. Hitler eyed Crete because it would provide the necessary airfields to support their war effort in North Africa. The Germans would later bomb Crete, targeting vital areas of infrastructure, mostly airports and harbors. Rumors spread of a German invasion, and it was not a question of *if*, but *when* and, more importantly, *how* and *where*.

One day, my father and I were working in our vineyards, spraying the fields. It was May 20, 1941. We had harnessed our spraying equipment to our backs and were walking up and down spraying the vines. Across from us, about two miles away, there was a hill; and behind the hill was the airport of Heraklion, the biggest city in Crete.

We observed two German planes, flying very low, almost touching the tops of the trees; they were coming toward us. We probably looked like soldiers with backpacks, and they flew closer and started to fire at us. The shots were so loud they sounded like a thousand balloons bursting at the same time as the bullets were hitting the leaves and the ground. Fortunately for us, their first strafing was not accurate, missing my father and me while we ran for cover. Shaken and thankful that we were all right, we were surprised to see that the planes had turned around to try another attack, heading straight for us. I quickly yelled to my father to remove the spraying equipment and take cover in a nearby ditch. By the time they started the second strafing, I had just barely made it into the ditch, and I could feel the bullets striking the ground by my shoes as loud machine gun fire came closer and closer to us. Fortunately, we survived the attack. We suspected that something big was going to happen next, and as we were gathering our equipment to return to our village, we witnessed hundreds of multicolored parachutes falling in the vicinity of the Heraklion airport, which was just outside the island's largest city and behind the hill in front of us. Since the Germans were landing only a few miles from us, we started to rush to our village, Archanes, which was in the opposite direction. Not too far from our vineyards was the ancient palace at Knossos, seat of the Minoan civilization and at which Sir Arthur Evans, the famous British archaeologist, had been excavating recently. All the villagers in our hometown were listening to the reports of an invasion on the radio, and the reports were that German paratroopers were landing all over the island. Most of us knew that there were no considerable Greek forces on Crete since they had been fighting in northern Greece and they were still there. There were reports of fierce resistance to the German invasion, and by the end of their initial attack, the Germans had lost about 1,500 paratroopers. By the third day, however, Hitler's elite paratroopers, the Fallschirmjager, had lost over half of the 8,000 sent in to capture Crete. How could this tiny island resist so defiantly? The German high command, not to be thwarted, responded by bombing the major cities on the island in preparation for another invasion. The Cretan resistance, along with Australian and New Zealand troops, nearly fought this one off; but the German's were able to secure Maleme airport on the far side of the island, allowing the German's to fly in reinforcements. The Cretan men, women, and children who fought bravely, along with the British troops, held out for approximately ten days.

The Germans, who were quite upset about their losses, naturally wanted to avenge their brothers-in-arms. This they did visciously against the civilian population that participated in the invasion. Their revenge was carried out in barbaric fashion as the Germans would kill civilians and burn villages suspected of complicity. In response to the German brutality, the Greek civilians formed resistance groups, which were aligned with the English Secret Intelligence Service, the SOE. The English were dedicated to resisting the Germans as much as the Greeks were, and after the fall of the island, a few of these SOE operatives stayed behind, so-called sleeper cells, to help organize resistance in the cities and in the mountainous regions where it would be more difficult for the Gestapo to find them.

My brother George and I had not forgotten that we were Americans, emigrating to Crete at an early age. We especially enjoyed speaking to the English soldiers, billeted not too far from us, prior to the invasion of Crete. My brother, George, kept continuous contact with high-ranking English officers who requested George to organize an underground resistance organization and report to them. George then enlisted many friends and previous classmates, as well as me, into an organization that he headed, and he worked directly under the SOE. Later on he had befriended a member of the SOE, Captain Patrick Leigh Fermor and became a trusted associate. George was chief representative on the civilian side under Captain Fermor. Since George was so well known, it was expected soon that someone would say something to the Germans.

Two years had passed since the Germans had invaded Crete in 1941, and by 1943, we were informed that the Gestapo had learned about the connection between my brother's organization and the SOE. A message, using a wireless, was sent to Cairo with a request to evacuate us from Crete before it was too late. The danger was obvious to all that resistance members would be tortured and killed, as well as their families. My brother, George, notified me and a few others that we should leave Heraklion; I received the notification while I was in my hometown, Archanes, and I told my parents that they had to be brave and accept the necessary departure of both of us, from the island of Crete. It was not easy for my parents to accept that the Gestapo wanted their sons, and both of them would have to leave the island of Crete to avoid capture. My parents started to cry at the possibility they may not see their children for a long time or maybe never again.

It was only a matter of time before the German police would come and ask my parents about their sons, especially my brother whose reputation as a leader of a big organization, was given over to the Gestapo by a traitor. This traitor had offered not to disclose the identity of my brother for a million drachmas.

I told my parents to say that we both wanted to go to Athens to college and went there only a few days. Later my father had a gun put to his head by a Gestapo officer asking him to tell the whereabouts of his son George. My father replied. "Sir, . . . you are an officer of the Gestapo, do you really believe that a twenty-one years old boy could ever be a leader of such a thing, as you say? On the island of Crete we have hundreds of high ranking military officers and you believe a boy leads such an organization? It must be a false accusation by someone who does not like my son!"

The Gestapo officer listened carefully to what my father said, thought for a while and told my father to go.

As I was having my last lunch with my father in our house, my mother sewed our birth certificates inside the lining of our jackets. She said it might be useful in Egypt to prove our American citizenship to the Americans. On the other hand, if we were stopped and searched for any reason by the Germans, and they found the birth certificates in the lining of our clothing that would be enough evidence for our execution.

George Doundoulakis with Captain Patrick Lee Fermor, 1942, of the SOE, before our evacuation to Egypt.

Loading my clothes on my bicycle and while saying goodbye with tears, the front door opened and a retired Colonel, Antonios Betinakis, who belonged to my brother's organization appeared. At least twice a week, he was giving me information or instructions to take to Heraklion for my brother, who would then pass this information on to the English. As soon as he saw me he was happy to have caught me in time. "Please, Helias," he said, "take this letter to your brother; it contains very important plans and be very careful with it since it contains names of new associates." I put the letter inside the hollow end of the right-sided handle bar leaving about a half an inch outside for easy access and I covered the end with the rubber grip. He must have approved my transportation method and told me: "Bravo Helias, very smart idea, nobody would ever suspect that inside the handle bar of the bicycle there are secret documents. You are a top-notch messenger Helias, that is why you are trusted with important and secret documents." And then he turned and with a passionate and sincere expression told my parents that they should be proud of their two sons fighting for the cause of freedom.

My mother, with tears in her eyes, replied; "Colonel Betinakis, I hope God is watching my sons because the freedom you are talking about might come with a high price."

I did not want to tell the Colonel that my brother and I were planning to leave the island of Crete but I knew my brother had left somebody else in charge and the Colonel's letter would identify him.

As I biked along, a German soldier whom I had spoken to in German often, was sitting with another group of soldiers by the high school, and yelled out "Helias, Halt." I had no intentions of stopping, so as I pedaled faster, he ran faster yet, and grabbed the bicycle so that the grip came off, and while the German was holding the rubber grip, the colonel's letter protruded from the handle. I immediately saw that he was sorry for what he did, and he tried to put the grip on himself, but I calmly took it from his hands and place it on the handle myself. I then sped toward Androulakis' house with the apologetic German behind me. Androulakis' house was our headquarters.

I stared into the fireplace at Androulakis' house wondering how it might have turned out if the German discovered the letter. He just wanted me to slow down, and it seemed like I could have exposed the entire organization.

(Five months later Colonel Betinakis, together with the mayor of the city of Heraklion and ten prominent citizens were shot by firing squad as retribution for sabotages done in and around Heraklion.)

"Helias" my brother said, "make sure there is nothing left in the house. Androulakis and Michael Kokkinos had to bury the explosives we hid in the fireplace at the Knossos Excavation Site."

Again we looked around the house, in case we had forgotten anything suspicious and after we were sure the house was clean we said good-bye to Androulakis' mother, and left. We were very lucky, though, since we had left in the nick of time just before the Germans had arrived. We hardly had gone a few blocks from the house when the Gestapo came and raided that house, turning everything upside down to look for us or any evidence of the organization's existence. The German Police put a gun to the head of Androulakis's mother, demanding the whereabouts of her son John, and George, my brother. She never broke. Thank God.

Having learned of the Gestapo's raid on the Androulakis house, we knew that we had to leave the island.

We walked for half a day before we reached a town called Saint Miron. I was told to stay in the mayor's house for about a week or ten days. At the end of the first week some curious neighbors thought I was the son of a famous partisan leader named Petrakogiorgis. Fearing for his family and his village, the mayor told me to leave before the Germans found out whom they were protecting in their house. Though I was not the son of that partisan leader and I told them so, I understood their concern, since his family would be killed and the house burned. Though I was not whom they thought I was, I was wanted by the German Police, anyway. The mayor, whose name was Dramatinos, telephoned someone he knew, and after a day and a half, a man came to escort me through the mountains of Crete. The guide and I left the village on foot, traveling through the Cretan mountains for about a day. We reached the town of Anogia, famous for their brave men, and stayed in the mayor's house for a few days. We were told that the mayor was the richest in that town, the owner of extensive tracts of land and sheep and employed many shepherds to take care of them. He sheltered and fed the partisans, besides our group and also SOE members, very often. At least one lamb was killed every day to feed his visitors. There, in the mayor's house I met with Patrick Leigh Fermor, the SOE representative and with five others from our

(Months after we had left Crete the Germans learned about the Mayor's help to SOE members and partisans and they came to the town, killed the Mayor and burned his house.)

organization. To repay part of the mayor's hospitality we took his brother to Egypt, by order of Patrick Leigh Fermor.

From Anogia, me, John Androulakis, and a guide, travelled to a cave on the lower hills of Mount Ida, the highest mountain on Crete (called Psiloritis by the Greeks). We stayed in that cave for at least ten days with very little food and water until we were informed that a torpedo boat was scheduled to pick up our group in two and half days. A guide took us and went to another cave nearby where we met with more people of our organization, and after counting, I realized we were sixteen people all together. There we were introduced to a new guide, who was a tall young man with a black scarf on his head and dressed in traditional Cretan baggy trousers and high black boots, and had a long knife tucked into his sash. With a very impressive expression, large black eyes, and bushy eyebrows, he explained to us that he alone knew the area we were going to go through. He was a large man with an equally large handlebar mustache in typical Cretan style. He said the travel was not going to be an easy one, and we would have to travel forty kilometers to the south shore of the island by foot. He then looked at each of us carefully and sternly warned us about the Germans, who were looking for us, and told us that the journey would be over the mountains in the dark. He told us that traveling by night would be our only hope of escaping. He warned us that in order to cover the twenty kilometers per night in the mountains, we would have to move fast, and sometimes run. The guide, who was a shepherd and was familiar with traveling through the mountains, wondered if we could possibly follow him? I was confident that I could. After all, I was only nineteen. But one of the others, a fifty-year-old man named Kastrinogiannis, a chemical engineer, was city folk and not accustomed to the ways of the mountain folk, let alone running in the dark. Could he keep up with the group? I wondered to myself since I felt he might not make it, and we talked about it, half joking with the others. The shepherd didn't take a liking to the humor and issued all of us a warning that no one could be left behind, and that he was instructed to kill anyone too weak to keep up with the rest. He had to make sure the Germans did not capture any of us at any cost because he might divulge the group's departure position and time. I was wearing a pair of old English army boots, which had no soles but the rubber from tires cut in the shape of the boot and tied to the boot with thin metal wire. I was worried that the wire would break if I put too much stress on the boot. More worrisome was the possibility of running in these boots without making a sound. Fortunately, we had no time to worry any more, and the guide instructed us to line up in a single file and follow him on our journey. He glanced at my shoes and sort of looked at me and said, "if your shoes fall apart, you won't be left behind. Either you'll run barefoot, or I'll kill you."

I put a few clothes and my jacket in my small bag which I slung across my back. I felt for the birth certificate that my mother had sewn into the lining of my jacket; it documented that I was born on July 12, 1923, in Canton, Ohio. As a result, I was very careful not to lose my jacket because it may be useful when I got to Cairo, Egypt. I thought the American authorities would be generous to an American citizen. At this time, I had no idea about the American secret service or the OSS. Just before dusk, the guide called everybody to get ready and form a line, one behind the other. We were also told that during the next five to six hours no one was allowed to talk or smoke because it would give up the group's position. We initially started out jogging on small paths, but our shepherd guide was trying to save time by using shortcut mountain routes, jumping like a wild goat across the rocky mountain terrain. The other young guys like me had no problem keeping up with the guide. The fifty-year-old chemist, Kastrinogiannis, was visibly affected, with his tongue hanging out, breathing with difficulty. When Kastrinogiannis asked the guide for a five-minute rest, the guide replied, "I have no time to spare. We have to make it to the next secure area by daybreak, which is fifteen kilometers away." The chemist did not repeat the request and remembered the warning issued earlier about preserving the group's rendezvous point with the English torpedo boat. The guide also mentioned that very soon from that point, the group would have to come down from the mountainous terrain and travel on the flat roads. Since these roads led toward the Timbaki airport, it was known for German patrol units guarding the area twenty-four hours a day while powerful searchlights moved over the whole area. We had to be careful to cross the heavily patrolled area in the next few hours before daybreak. In a short time, we realized that we were going downhill and saw the searchlight moving around the area in the distance. Our guide instructed us to move across the main road, a road that I reasoned was a main route toward the airfield, and likely heavily guarded. The whole time I maintained a close distance to the guide for fear of becoming separated from him, and knowing that we had to cross the main road frightened me. The thought of becoming separated struck me with fear, so much so that I tried extra hard to stay on his heels and not at the end of the line where I could get lost or be left behind. All the while, I was still trying to keep my boots from falling apart. As we were approaching the main road, and before we were able to cross it, the guide noticed that a patrol car was coming, and he told us to jump into a ditch that ran parallel to the road. He lifted his index finger to his lips in the "Be quiet" gesture and closed his eyes, meaning "Not even a breath." How could I do this? I was just running at full speed to keep up with this damned fool, and now no moving, breathing . . . I just closed my eyes. But as luck would have it, I made a sudden move, and the wire holding my right boot together fell apart. My foot came right through the bottom of the boot! I tried to wrap another wire around my boot and leather sole, but I realized that now I was last in line! *Oh my God,* I thought, *my worst nightmare has come true!* I saw the German patrol's searchlight approaching us, and I was still barefoot. I tried to run, but I had to jump back into the ditch as the searchlight once again passed over me. Now, not only was I last in line, but I was also falling behind the group. I was in danger of being caught. What could be worse, I thought? Once in the ditch and motionless—feeling tired, hungry, and thirsty—my mind and body needed to sleep for we had been on the run, it seemed, for eons. So the unexplainable happened, and I dozed off and dreamt about my home that I had left; and the dreams were so vivid about my parents, my friends, conflicting with the body's inexorable desire to sleep.

As soon as the patrol car left the scene, the guide must have signaled the group to cross the main road, but since I had fallen behind and fallen asleep, I did not hear it. Maybe it was God's will to make me wake up as the patrol passed, or just maybe in my dreams, I heard a car speed by; but just then, I woke up and saw that I was alone. I started to sweat at the prospect of losing the group, falling asleep again, and getting caught by the next patrol. They would execute me, for sure, or not until they first beat me and until I told them why I had been alone near the airport, a forbidden area, far from my home with an American birth certificate hidden in my jacket. They would surely guess that I had lost my group, and I, the straggler, would pay the price. As I was imagining my capture by the Germans, I happened to be staring hard in the direction the group was headed prior to losing them, and I saw something move in the dark, which looked like a man running; or maybe it was a German soldier on patrol. I couldn't be sure. Maybe it was someone from our group who also became separated, for why should I be the only one to have fallen asleep? After all, Kastrinogiannis had been poked fun of, the old guy, maybe it was him whom I saw in the dark, running to catch up with the others. It was probably wishful thinking, or was I again fortunate to be on the right side of this war? I didn't know, but I felt no more secure where I was, so off I went. I had to go toward the moving object, and there was no other alternative. I had no time to worry about my shoes, so I took off the other shoe and put them in my pack and started running entirely barefoot, as fast as I could. Although I was stepping on thorns and sharp stones, my fear did not allow me to feel anything, which was the same fear that caused me to fall asleep and made me forget about everything I was thinking about. My sleep-deprived body was now put to the test. I was running fast, but someone ahead of me was moving faster, and since it was not getting closer, I concluded it must be one of our group and not a German. Who else would be running like a demon in the dead of night? I decided to run even faster since my feet had gotten used to the rough terrain, and I was able to get close enough to recognize that it was indeed someone from our group. I soon came close enough to be considered the last runner in line and part of the group again. My joy at seeing this straggler was too much, and I couldn't bear it any longer. I cried while running, but no one even turned around to see me coming. If I had gotten lost, nobody would ever have known it until we were on the beaches. They all had their problems trying to keep up the pace, especially since our so-called guide cared for nobody but himself. I decided not to tell anyone why I fell behind because there would be little or no sympathy for me from the rest of the group. If I had not been awakened in time and unable to rejoin the group, they would be in jeopardy, including my brother. I did not see him checking to see if his younger brother was in the group after we had crossed the road, when the searchlights were above us. Obviously, he was looking out for himself too, as we all were. Even while having those thoughts in my mind, I still said to myself I should keep quiet. They wouldn't trust me again for the remainder of the trip, so I could not tell anyone what happened to me, not even my brother.

After two nights of running, my feet were bleeding from cuts and scrapes; and now, utterly exhausted, hungry, and thirsty, we started going downhill. At daybreak, we saw the sea behind the trees. I smelled the salt air and the distinctive smell of the ocean. We eventually saw the shore, which meant that our goal was in sight. The guide told us that after we got closer to the shore we would hide under the trees or behind large rocks along the shore and wait until the following night for the torpedo boat to come pick us up. He also told us to be aware of the German patrol post on the top of a nearby hill, which afforded the Germans an excellent vantage point overlooking the shoreline, and not to talk or smoke before the rendezvous. Because this stretch of sand was unobstructed and might be used for amphibious assaults on the island, it was monitored continuously by the Germans. The instructions were clear: "No smoking, no talking, just try to sleep." We had arrived at daybreak, and the English torpedo boat was scheduled to arrive the following night at 0100 hours.

The rendezvous was about twenty hours away, and we had not eaten anything from the previous day and the meal we had consisted of only a piece of bread and perhaps a handful of olives. The next twenty hours would be without food and possibly no water until the evacuation. How then could we sleep with hunger pangs and the added fear that the Germans might ambush us at any moment? I spotted a small broad-leafed tree standing next to a big grayish white boulder and went to sit under it. I thought this would make a nice place to sleep in the next twenty hours, so I piled up some of the fallen leaves for a mattress and a smooth stone became my pillow. I had just laid down and closed my eyes when I sensed that I was being watched. A greenish yellow lizard that came from under the rock stared at me, opening and closing its eyes, wondering if I was planning to be there permanently. Perhaps, I thought, I had taken its rock. I moved my hand in a "Get away" gesture, and it ran and hid under the big rock. At least against the lizard, I had won.

The sun rose; and with dawn's sunlight, I could see most of the others spreading all around me, each having found their own makeshift bed. Fifteen hours to go, and I thought, *God, if only for today, you could make this sunrise a sunset.* I observed also that the sun seemed to be moving very slowly that morning. And I wanted to stand up and say to the group, "Even the sun rises slower today, fellows. How could we sleep hungry, also with the sun shining on our eyes?" **And the most important, who's on watch for a possible German patrol coming while we all are supposed to be motionless or asleep?**

I must have been too weak to comprehend anything further. After two nights of running, I was exhausted and hungry, and I fell asleep.

Obviously, I had no choice but to give up to fate, and if we were destined to be found out by the Germans, we could not protect ourselves anymore. We had reached the end of our destination. I thought as the Italians say, "Que sera sera!"

When I woke up, I noticed the sun was now peeking out from behind the trees in the western sky. It was late afternoon, and I was asleep for the whole day, and fear gripped me. Was I all alone, or were the others still around me? With difficulty, I raised my head; and with great satisfaction, I spotted my roommate, the lizard who, by its expression was sure that I had become a permanent co-resident of the boulder. And to my blessed surprise, I waved to John Androulakis, and he returned a wave and a smile. Remembering the guide's warning about a German post on the top of the next hill, I did not talk. I did not get up to talk to John, and I knew he was doing the same, and each one of us was trying to make the best of it for the remaining five to six hours.

At twilight, the shepherd guide came over to the group and in a hushed voice said that we should make our way over to the large rocks by the water's edge and creep down low until the boat arrived. Our waiting was now down to a few hours. I imagined a big loaf of bread with some cheese and a large pitcher of water. This would have been an ideal supper; I did not think of big dinners. Though I must have been hallucinating, I realized it would not appear.

These remaining hours were the hardest and seemed to linger on and on. In order to ignore my weakness and hunger, I reminisced about my parents, who must have been sure by now that we were enjoying the Cairo nightlife. After all, almost one month had passed since our farewell, and yet we hadn't left Crete. If they only knew that we were crouching behind some rocks on Crete's southern shore, and that we had gone through these unbelievably dangerous and unsparing days.

Finally midnight approached. All were watching the moonless beach, vigilant to an approaching vessel. But to our disappointment, 0130 hours passed, then 0200 hours, then 0300 hours, and still no boat. We started to worry that if the boat did not come by daybreak, what would we do? There was no turning back. Our shepherd guide would not know where to take us, and might we need to return to our cave hideout in the mountains without my shoes? I shuddered at the thought. I also didn't forget that we were on the run from the Germans and could not go back anywhere. The Gestapo was looking for us, and no one could offer us shelter. At that disposition I could only think to pray: God! Please help us!

While the entire group of sixteen helpless people was silent and expressionless, staring at each other with the same questions in their minds and obviously praying, too, at 0330 hours I noticed two tall people headed toward the shore. One of them was my brother George and Patrick Leigh Fermor who were signaling to something they must have seen. I then could distinguish a moving object in the water headed to the shoreline, which we could make out to be a rubber dinghy; and as it came closer, it became clear that it was manned by two sailors, rowing very slowly and purposefully. The dinghy was tethered to a long rope that led out to sea, which was attached to the torpedo boat obviously anchored offshore. The sailors attached the other end to a large boulder on shore. They used the rope to pull the dinghy back and forth to the torpedo boat, carefully avoiding any splashes that the oars would have made.

"Four people at a time," they whispered. When my turn came to go, I turned around, bade farewell, and thanked Captain Fermor, whose message had sent the torpedo boat. I also didn't forget our guide who brought us to safety; and I realized that although he was a stern and cold man, it was to his credit that we had made it through this harrowing week, and that he had completed his mission successfully. I shook his hand and said we would meet again when the war was over. He nodded and turned away.

As I thought it was my turn to go, three, not two, sailors now occupied the returning dinghy. Surprised, a tall man stepped off the dinghy, waded to shore, and was welcomed by Captain Lee Fermor and the shepherd guide with warm embraces and the two-cheeked kiss typical of the Greeks. I later was told that this was the famous partisan leader, Petrakogiorgis. I almost went to tell him that I was mistaken for his son at St. Miron, but I let him go.

Then I saw the three walking away and they disappeared into the night.

I sat in the boat and stared into the darkness at the shores of Crete, wondering when I would return.

(It would take me twenty seven years to return to Crete, for unjustified reasons. After the war, Greece demanded that my brother George and I go and serve in the Greek army. We told them that we were American citizens and that we already had served in the American army, that we had been decorated by both the American and Greek governments. Greece insisted that since we grew up in Greece, we were Greek citizens and that we should fulfill our obligations in the Greek army.)

As we approached the torpedo boat, which was at least fifty feet long, we were assisted in climbing aboard by grinning English sailors who instructed us to move quietly to the bow, to sit down and dangle our legs off the deck, and to hold on tight to the ropes that ringed the bow of the boat. The boat's engines were at a low throttle, and the muffled engines could not be heard over the waves and wind of the sea. Once all were on deck, the boat took up anchor quietly, heading due south; and once out of this restricted area, the captain increased its speed gradually to the point that we were flying over the waves.

We told our English rescuers that we had not eaten for over two days, so they brought us all they had: canned beef hash. Our stomachs were so empty, and as we ate the food very fast while the boat was traveling at high speed over rough seas, I began to wretch violently, the vomitus going all over our clothes.

Our luck of having escaped I thought did not last as a German patrol plane spotted us at daybreak and flew down low to see who we were. After making two low circles around us, the plane returned and headed back toward Crete. General quarters were called, and the English sailors immediately went to their deck gun positions, waiting for a squadron of attack planes to appear. The danger of being on deck during an attack meant that we might be the first to be killed if the planes returned. After all the effort to escape the island, it did not seem right to be killed at this point. The crew decided to increase speed and further the distance between the boat and the shore, and that made it even harder to hold on to the ropes in front of the boat. We were exhausted for over an hour as we pulled the ropes down when the boat was going up to the top of the waves, and then pushed the ropes up when the boat was going down. The intensity of the situation lasted about an hour, and since no airplanes returned, the gunners left their battle positions and took their helmets off. We all breathed a deep sigh of relief and a breath of fresh air. By early afternoon that day, we could see the shoreline of Africa. There were no trees as far as we could see, only sand as we approached the Libyan shoreline. The boat entered the harbor and docked, and we were told to wash up and shave. It was the first time we looked in the mirror for about a week, and we did not recognize ourselves. We all looked like hermits with beards and long hair and, of course, we were sick. The English gave us new clothes and told us to throw away our old ones in a big barrel. When I was ready to throw my shoes in the barrel, I turned to a British sergeant who was next to me and showed him the old army boot with the rubber sole kept on with plain wires. I told him how far I had traveled with these boots. He could not believe it and told me to keep it as a reminder of my ordeal. I replied, "To tell you the truth, I feel as if I should do that." And I held them in my hands for a few seconds, remembering the hard times and the service they had given me, and tossed them out. After we had cleaned, shaved, and put on British uniforms, we realized the transformation the group had gone through. "Just a short time ago, our tired bodies could have been left to rot in some ditch or to be tortured by the Gestapo or even to be eaten by sharks", one said.

We were told to go eat in an army cafeteria. The attendant in charge told us that it was not time for dinner and that there was no food ready to be served. He did offer us some bread, butter, and jam. Originally he'd brought us five loaves of bread, but they were devoured in seconds. He brought another five loaves of bread, and these were also devoured as quickly. At a nearby table, some English soldiers witnessed this spectacle, so they brought us the bread from their table. They asked us where we were from. We had told them we had not eaten anything for almost three days, and they felt sorry for us.

They said that if they knew we were coming they would have saved something for us.

After we had eaten enough bread, we were told that we would have to sleep in the camp and that the following morning, we would have to go to Cairo, Egypt. We were in Marsa Matruh, Libya. The distance between the two places was six hundred kilometers. The transportation available was two open army trucks, which had nothing to sit on except some small wooden boxes on the truck floor. That trip had appeared to be another painful journey, so I found a wooden box and tested it out; after all, sitting on a wooden box would be better than sitting on the open truck's floor. Once on the truck, it seemed that the ride was going to be rough. We were going to go not sixty but six hundred kilometers. When we started speeding down that straight road, the truck was traveling about one hundred and fifty kilometers per hour, and with the slightest pressing of the brakes, the boxes we were sitting on were sliding all over the truck, hitting the other boxes that the other guys were sitting on. All of us were suffering the same fate. "My god," we all said, "is there anything else that we have to go through until we reach our destination?" Everywhere we looked, as far as we could see, there was nothing but sand. We literally were in the middle of the desert. The road was obviously built on the sand, and for many miles, it was perfectly straight, so the driver was pushing the truck to the limit.

After a very long and boring drive through the desert, we noticed something that looked like trees in the distance. "It must be an oasis," we all said, and we were right. The driver said we were approaching the delta of the Nile, which provides fruits and vegetables for almost all of Egypt.

After we had arrived in Alexandria, we rested a little; and after having some refreshments and a few Egyptian cigarettes, we left Alexandria and passed vineyards and gardens of many different types, lined with eucalyptus and palm trees along the road to Cairo.

Cairo was truly a different place. It amazed us all. We soon reached the city's outskirts where I saw trees and vegetation I had never seen on the island of Crete. Mimosa trees and their wispy pink and white flowers seemed to bloom everywhere. Their fragrance filled the air. We traveled through the streets, still on our truck, and noticed that the men were wearing white robes with tasseled red fezzes. And interestingly, the women wore black robes with a cloth, allowing others to see only their eyes. It was June 7, 1943, and the temperature was close to one hundred degrees Fahrenheit in the shade. I wondered, maybe the Egyptians were more comfortable than us, dressed as we were; even the children wore long robes. I assumed it must be a religious thing and thought that I was probably looking at fundamental Islam in Egypt. This country even had streetcars that ran on rails, many of which were so overcrowded that some passengers were riding outside the streetcar by hanging on to the windows so as not to pay the fare! It was my first time experiencing this form of transportation. The streets were lined with beautiful white and blue-awninged stores and sidewalk cafes. There were vendors of all kinds selling rose bouquets, kebobs, watches, and Turkish coffee. Small plazas built with both Byzantine and Ottoman designs seemed to spring up from nowhere and were packed with afternoon shoppers, both young and old. Large arched windows were a common facade along these streets. Cars were everywhere.

Distracted by Cairo's colorful streets, we hadn't realized that we were exiting Cairo again as if the driver wanted to give us a short sightseeing tour of Cairo before he went out into the desert again. Driving in the desert for a short time, we noticed that we were about to enter an English army base. We all thought it would be our home until our next assignment. The camp was located in and around nothing but desert with no trees; the temperature inside the barracks was over one hundred degrees, and it was dusty and very uncomfortable. For the first time, I dreamt of a rainy day and asked one of our Egyptian servants wearing a fez, "Has it rained here lately?" He told me, in his best English, that it had not rained in Cairo for ten years! I quickly told the others, who were equally disappointed.

On the third day there, as we were thinking and worrying about the very real possibility of staying in this place for a long time, a British sergeant came into the room, walking in front of a British officer. The sergeant slammed his foot down and raised his openhanded salute to his forehead in typical English fashion and announced the officer. He called out five names to report to HQ. They were George Doundoulakis, John Androulakis, two others, and mine. Then the sergeant saluted, reversed order, and left with the officer.

Chapter 3

- Resting period in Iliopolis, a suburb of Cairo where the officers of British intelligence resided
- Preparation by the SOE to send the Doundoulakis brothers back to western Crete
- Leaving the SOE to join OSS.

Leaving the British army base camp was a relief, especially when they told us to get our stuff and follow a certain person with a rank of sergeant.

He told us to enter a car, and then he told us that we would be going to a surprise. He said that we were either lucky or very important people and that we should wait and see.

We did not know what he meant, but we kept quiet and waited to see where he was taking us. We had a couple of bad surprises lately, so we just did not want to speculate on what kind of surprises we should expect. As the old Greek saying goes, after you've fallen a few times, you don't really mind falling again.

After leaving that miserable army camp in the desert it seemed that we were entering the suburbs of Cairo again, but this time, it was even prettier than before. We crossed a bridge and went into an area where every house was a villa, which the driver said was called Iliopolis. It was where the rich people lived; and as we were going, we stopped in front of a villa, and the sergeant said, "This is the surprise. This is your destination!"

(Later on we found out that Patrick Leigh Fermor, the English Captain we were working within Crete had made that recommendation, which was that we would be taken to live in that villa.)

"It is the villa utilized by the high officials of the English Intelligence Service," he said. "Since you were sent to live here, you must have been recommended by some very important person or you must be very important persons yourselves."

Two people who spoke in Greek welcomed us, and two Arabs helped us with our belongings. We entered the house, which had marble steps and glass doors. We were careful to walk on those corridors whose floor was covered with white marble tiles.

They showed us three bedrooms which could accommodate two people each. They showed us the dining room where we would be eating at tables all covered with white tablecloths. At suppertime that evening, two Arabs served us. The same service followed next day and every day thereafter with breakfast, lunch, and supper. We thought this extraordinary treatment would last only a few days, but we were told that we would stay a month or more till we were ready to be sent somewhere else.

We could not believe our eyes that we were here. And we considered ourselves lucky that we had been chosen to be resting in this luxurious villa. The remaining group of people with whom we left with from Crete, as we found out later on, were sent to the Greek army station in the Middle East.

The following day after we had arrived, we realized that two blocks from the villa we were staying in was a train station, and we could hear the train passing, a train taking people to Cairo. As we had been told, the villa was in a suburb called Iliopolis; so the next day, Androulakis said to me, *Let's go to Cairo.* We walked to the station, and without noticing what stop it was, we got on the train. As we were walking in Cairo's streets, we found Greek restaurants and met with many Greeks as well as Cretans. After two hours of admiring the center of Cairo, we decided to get on the train back to Iliopolis. As the train was leaving, we remembered that we did not know where to get off. Also, we had not written the address of the villa. We had no telephone; we did not know the area of Iliopolis we were living in. As the train moved along the tracks, we tried to recognize the stop but all looked the same to us. At one stop, John said he thought that we should get off; but I said no, and without hesitation, John jumped out, and the train left with me on it. At the next stop, I got out and tried to recognize buildings, but to me they all looked the same. A policeman saw me looking around and came to me. I was dressed as a British soldier but had no identification, and I did not know where I was going or living. Since my English was just okay, and the policeman did not understand what I was saying, he called another policeman, and it seemed that, they wanted to take me to the police station.

Though I did not know the address of the house I wanted to go to, at least I remembered that across the street, I had noticed a church; so I kept repeating to the policemen, "Church, a church." As the policemen were hesitating on what to do with me and were looking at each other a well-dressed man, who curiously approached us, heard "Church, church" and told the policemen that he knew where there was a church two blocks away; and he volunteered to take me to the church.

Obviously, the policemen did not care to solve my situation anymore or to bother taking me to the police station, and since I was dressed as an English soldier, they had no right to hold me. They told me to follow the man to the church. As I was walking with the man, I was very doubtful if he was taking me where I wanted to go or somewhere else; but I had no other choice except to follow him. We walked about two blocks, and the man, at a certain point, said, "Here is the church." To my surprise, when I turned my head and looked across the street, I saw the villa. I thanked the man profusely, and I went to the entrance. By this time, it was very late. It was past 1:00 AM, and the door was closed; but I noticed someone was in the office, so I waved at him. And he came and opened the door. When I went to our bedroom, I noticed that John had not gotten back yet. Obviously, he must have had more difficulty in finding the villa, I said to myself since it was past 2:00 AM when he finally entered the bedroom. His adventures must be even more interesting than mine, I said to myself. But it should be heard next day, so I pretended I was asleep and kept quiet. The next day he told me how he paid for his impulsivity, and should have listened to me.

We stayed in that villa for over two and a half months and the neighbors, whom we supposed to be rich, were wondering who we were. Though we were dressed like soldiers, we did not behave like soldiers. We were idle, not working, and at night we'd find the local nightclubs after which you'd find us singing Greek love songs on the street corners to the passing girls. They probably thought we were rich; they envied us, and because it was always hot, we used to sleep with the balcony door open all the time. One night while we were sleeping, thieves came in and took everything they could find—watches, wallets, even shoes, and clothes. They were so professional that some watches were taken from our wrists and wallets were taken out from our trousers pockets without anyone waking up. The English sergeant also said "Too bad they didn't leave their names; they would have made good spies."

We had the time of our lives in that villa, and we did anything we wanted to do; we probably couldn't ask for more gracious hosts. Since everything good does not last forever, the time came for us also to repay the English for the good times we had enjoyed.

We realized that unusual meetings by officers were taking place in the villa's office, and we suspected that they were planning something for us.

In Cairo, Egypt, in British uniforms.
On the left, John Androulakis, author at right.

We were right to suspect that our good times were coming to an end, and the first to be called in was John Androulakis. After he came out, he told us he was going to be sent on a mission but that he was told to keep it secret for security reasons. We wished him good luck as he departed the following day. We learned later on that John was to guide a group of English commandos to Crete on a mission to destroy oil tanks and ammunition in Peza, Crete. He was told that the only thing he would have to do was to guide the group of six commandos to the location of the sabotage. After landing in the south shore of Crete he was to take them to Peza and, after the sabotage, to lead them to the south shore again for evacuation.

John took the group to the proper area, and as the English commandos saw the double barbed wires and fences and the German guards, they became hesitant and refused to go since they felt that it would be impossible for six commandos to enter that carefully patrolled area and not be noticed. John told them that they had only a couple of hours to do the sabotage before daylight. In the time of hesitation and refusal, since John felt responsible for the success or failure of the mission, he decided that he could perform the sabotage by himself even though he would only do a portion of what was originally planned. Since the area was so well guarded, if all the commandos took part, they would be discovered and maybe all would be killed. But if one person went in, he would have a greater chance not to be discovered, so John loaded himself with time bombs, and he slipped into the forbidden area. All that time, the English commandos watched John from behind.

Crawling slowly on the ground, he reached one pile of oil tanks and put a couple of time bombs on them. Then he started going toward the other pile of oil tanks, but he had difficulty crossing an open area because of passing guards, and thus he was delayed. The first pile started exploding. The Germans, thinking it was an air raid, started firing their antiaircraft guns. After they realized it had been a sabotage, the German guards came, looking for the saboteurs; but John was able to escape from the forbidden area, rejoin with the group, and was able to escape and lead them to the south shore of Crete for evacuation.

The next group to be called by the officers of the English Intelligence in the office of the villa was my brother and me. Obviously, the officers had planned a mission for us, but before they started describing the mission, my brother surprised them by telling them of our desire to be introduced to the American secret service, called OSS.

My brother told them that we were American citizens and had with us our birth certificates to prove it, that we would prefer that we get introduced to the OSS. Immediately the English officers objected to George's proposal, saying that the English had done so much for us but we did not seem to have appreciated it, and that when the time came to repay them at the time they needed us, we wanted to desert them and go to OSS.

Then my brother told them that they should not consider it a desertion. We had appreciated their hospitality tremendously especially during this resting period, but the OSS was a similar organization to English Intelligence, and since both organizations worked for the same cause against the Germans and we were American citizens, why not let us serve with the Americans?

The English officers, seeing our logical and proper inclination to be members of the OSS, must have notified the OSS office in Cairo because in no time, an OSS officer got in touch with us, invited us to join him, and came and took us to the OSS headquarters in Cairo. Obviously, the English officers must have told them of the vital underground role we had played in Crete working for English Intelligence, and they could not wait to have us join their organization. When we reached the OSS headquarters, we entered three barbed wire gates with a guard, which gave us the impression that we were in a very secure organization.

They took us to a room where other officers waited for us with big smiles and lots of handshakes. From what they had heard about us, we were what they were looking for. We were American citizens, and they could trust us. We knew Greek and had no accent. And a very important factor—we had experience and were willing to go back to Greece. The commanding officer mentioned that though we were American citizens, we would be classified as civilians working for the OSS.

The 2 American born brothers emigrated to Greece in 1925.
Helias at the age of two George at the age of 4

The two brothers at the early public school grades

Chapter 4

- Enlistment in the American army and immediate assignment into SI, the Secret Intelligence section of the OSS

The OSS officers were extremely eager to assign us to the organization, but to them the easiest way was that we volunteered as civilians.

Two brothers first day of enlistment in the U.S. Army

My brother, George, replied very smartly that since we were American citizens and we had our birth certificates to prove it, we would have liked to become American soldiers. The commanding officer replied that it was impossible since to become an American soldier, we needed basic training, and we had no time for that back in United States.

My brother said that we only needed secret service training, not basic training; and for that, we already had the underground experience.

My brother also, seeing how urgently they needed us, pressed them more by saying that if we had to stay as civilians, we might as well go back with the British.

When they heard that, they called the Pentagon in Washington DC; and within twenty-four hours, they got the permission to enlist us in the American army without basic training.

They assigned two officers to help us go through the particulars in the enlistment, namely, health examinations, the swearing in, uniforms, and other paperwork.

Not only had we become American soldiers but, having heard from the British about my brother's achievements, they gave him a rank of staff sergeant—a rank that a regular American soldier with basic training would have to work hard for a couple of years to get. My brother became staff sergeant overnight. They also made me corporal, and I felt very proud of that promotion. After we were given American uniforms to wear and after we put our stripes on, we looked in the mirror and could not believe the transformation we had gone through.

From Cretan villagers, we had become English soldiers; and now we had turned into American soldiers. From all these three changes, if anyone looked at our faces, he would notice now that we were content, we were happy and proud to be in this final stage.

We knew, though, that by having received all this attention, we would have the obligation to repay them by doing the service they urgently needed from us. They needed to send people in operative positions to act as spies in Greece, and they knew we were qualified. After enlistment in the American army, we were told by the officers in charge that we had been transferred immediately to OSS and that we should be taken to the OSS spy training school.

One lieutenant told us we were in store for something grand. It would be the school we would be taken to, but before we left the OSS headquarters, he said, "Why don't you take anything you like from the supply room? Free, of course," he said. "After all, you are newly inducted soldiers, and you deserve more." He took us to the supply room and said, "Get two more uniforms, more shoes, more underwear, cigarettes, candies, and whatever else you want." After each one of us had filled up one army bag, the lieutenant said, "Let's go to school."

Chapter 5

- Arrival at the "palace" spy school
- Five months of spy training
- Parachute jumping from various heights
- Morse code and wireless instruction and operation
- Commando training (defensive type)
- Environment assimilation
- Techniques in opening locks and safes in order to photograph or steal important documents
- Story fabrication and lying
- Methods of escaping if captured
- Elimination (how to kill in order to escape, if captured)

Having filled up one large army satchel with extra uniforms and clothing and various other items from the supply room, George and I followed the lieutenant to his car.

"Next stop, the spy school," the lieutenant said. "Let us go to the surprise, a place you'll always remember."

We got into the car, and we were still wondering what would that surprise be. We drove outward from Cairo, driving parallel to the river Nile in a beautiful area with villas and mansions on the opposite side of the river.

Suddenly the lieutenant stopped the car and told us, "Well, here is your school." We looked and saw a palace.

I looked in disbelief and told the lieutenant, "This is a school? This is a Sultan's palace!"

"Yes," he said, "it is a palace . . . it belongs to King Farouk's brother-in-law, who has three palaces. And obviously, he does not need this one that much and is renting it to the OSS. The OSS is using it as a training school to train spies. "How do you like it?" the lieutenant asked us again. We continued staring at it. It looked like a palace shown in fairy tales.

We drove up front, and as we got out from the car, we faced a tremendous entrance that led to an enclosed garden. As we walked toward the palace entrance, we went up a dozen or so marble steps. We slid open a large pocket door that was made of sculptured glass and wood, and after it was opened, it was hidden inside the wall. As we entered, we saw a colossal spiral staircase seen only in the movies. The lieutenant showed us some buttons on the wall, and if they were pressed, the partitions would move away and the entire first floor would be transformed into an enormous dance floor capable of accommodating over three hundred people. The floor designs had many colors of marble, no doubt works of art of famous artists. Going up to the second floor, the entire upstairs was separated into four completely individual apartments, each one with a different-colored marble; and each individual apartment area housed complete facilities of bedrooms, dressing rooms, and washrooms.

Our group of fifteen was divided into four groups so that each group was assigned a different-colored marble apartment. So if we were asked where we were staying, we would say pink, blue, white, or green. I was assigned in the pink-marbled apartment.

In the back of the house, there was also a tremendous garden with the most exotic trees we had seen. Under the house, the entire area was for the servants and also for the kitchen. On the other floors, there were playrooms, billiard and ping-pong rooms, exercise rooms, and lecture rooms.

In the dining room, the tables were covered with white tablecloths. Egyptian personnel prepared the food, but it was brought to the tables and served to us by American soldiers, one of whom was a sergeant. I found out later on that almost all the personnel were sons or relatives of congressmen who would rather have them be servants than be on the front line.

We realized that there were fifteen of us trainees, including my brother and myself; and all of us were to be trained to become spies, mostly Greeks. There were also two Yugoslavians and three Italians. There were thirty personnel for us fifteen trainees. The highest-ranking officer was Major Vassos, followed by two captains and four lieutenants. The remaining teaching personnel were at least sergeants.

We were told that the instruction would be seven hours every day, and afterward, we could go to Cairo using their own bus and return by the same bus on specified time schedules. We were forbidden to use taxis to return to school for safety reasons. We were told that before we joined the group, one student returned in a taxi and was dismissed. We did not really need to go to Cairo very often since the palace provided all types of entertainment, and we preferred to stay in the school area. Besides the school facilities across the street, there was the river Nile, whose banks offered a very desirable area for walking. No need to risk getting lost on a train again!

And as if we did not have enough of the many luxuries in the palace, we were also told that for OSS personnel only there was a 150-foot yacht in the river Nile, a short distance from the palace, which we could visit and entertain ourselves in. So on the second day, I was very anxious to see the yacht, and instead of going to Cairo, I decided to walk and visit the yacht. I showed my OSS identification and got in. Immediately, two Egyptians with white robes came to me and asked how they could entertain me. One Arab asked if I wanted to go for a sailboat ride, which I declined, and I realized he was disappointed since that must have been his job, while the other Arab asked if I wanted to dine in the yacht's dining room. I agreed, and while leading me to the dining room, he showed me the yacht and said I could sleep in any cabin if I wanted to.

I told him I would not be able to sleep in the yacht but that a supper would be enough. In the dining room, two waiters came to serve me. I felt that I was living in a different world, a world of luxury and fantasy and that my payoff time might be on my next mission.

In addition to all these luxuries in Cairo's center, American forces had rented a big hotel called the Grand Hotel, which was for Americans only. As American soldiers, we could go there anytime we wanted, and many times, I took some Cretans with me to play billiards or ping-pong.

One day the lieutenant, who had helped us during induction in the army, saw me in the dining room and asked if I was happy with what I had seen up to that time. "Of course, I am happy," I said to him. "But don't forget, I am still very confused of the change. I still don't believe people could live this way. I had just come from a little village in Crete, and my family was living in an old three-room house without plumbing or electricity. Even in winter, I had to go outside to wash myself or go to the toilet. And now I am living in the pink marble apartment of a palace?" He smiled, and he told me that he understood.

"Tomorrow," the lieutenant said, "I am going to get some ammunition from the U.S. army barracks. Would you like to come with me?" So next day we got in a car, and we went outside of Cairo. It looked like the desert. The temperature must have been over one hundred degrees, and we found all the American soldiers living in tents. They had no clothes from the middle and up, and they were glistening in the sun from their sweat-soaked bodies.

"Do you see where your fellow American soldiers are staying?" the lieutenant said to me, and I did not have to reply. I knew what he was trying to tell me, that I was treated differently from the others since they were expecting me to leave soon on my assignment, and with the high likelihood of getting captured or killed behind enemy lines.

The time came for us to start the training, and some of us were gathered in the lecture hall.

"The first classifications for some of you will be parachutes and commando training, and for that," the major said, "you will be sent to Haifa, Palestine, to join the English commando training group there." We had not been more than a week to ten days in the palace when we were told that we would leave for Palestine the following day. "I know," the major said. "You love it here in the palace, but after a couple of weeks, you will be back here. After all," he said, "no matter where you will be sent, your base is here in the palace."

True enough, the next morning, some of us departed for Palestine and went straight to parachute-jumping training camp. Since that camp was very big, they split our group, and each one of us went in a different jumping group. It happened that I was the only American in a group of about twelve soldiers, mostly English, assigned a certain airplane. Each group had a sergeant in charge whom we followed for various prejumping instructions. The sergeant said that the parachute jumping course would take about ten days. The first four days we would exercise all day to make our bodies, as he said, very elastic. So we were running in the early morning, twice or more, around the entire airfield until we fell down with our tongues hanging out. We ate boiled squash and potatoes, so without exaggeration, in the ten days at this camp, I must have lost ten pounds. After six days of exhausting exercise, we were first trained how to turn when we hit the ground. For that they had a platform about seventy-five feet high, which you could reach by climbing a vertical ladder. On that small platform, the sergeant in charge would tie you with ropes similar to that of a parachute and push you out from the platform to start you swinging down that scary swing. And we were instructed that just before we reached the lowest point, we were to push a buckle and, as we were released from the ropes, to turn our bodies and roll over the ground. The swing would be similar to falling with a parachute; and that swing was so scary that I remember a middle-aged English captain who refused to go up to that swing. He said, "I will jump from the airplane, but I will not use the swing." We, the young guys, did not feel the danger so we thought we were in a playground and enjoyed even the "horror swing," as it was called.

After the first six days, having "softened our bones" as the sergeant used to say, we got in the plane. And they showed us how to clip our parachute bag on a cable, slide it toward the exit door, and, when the red light over the exit door turned green, to jump out as quickly as possible. We had been assigned numbers for each jump, and the first jump would have been from two thousand feet. "Any volunteers to be the first?" the sergeant asked. Since everyone was quiet, I raised my hand, and the sergeant acknowledged it.

He said that at the first jump we would fall on top of the airfield where there would be no trees, but on the other jumps, we would fall in areas with trees. He showed us how to pull the parachute ropes and which ones to pull in order to move the parachute sideways and fall between the trees. "You don't want to fall on the top of a one-hundred-foot-high tree and get stuck, would you?" he said.

A picture of the author at the parachute jumping schools.

Parachute Training in Palestine. (The author at right)

Being the first to jump made me feel like a leader. I was the number one man in a line of twelve others behind me. Then I thought of my friends in my village in Crete. If they could only see me leading a line of twelve parachutists ready to jump from a height of two thousand feet, what would they think? How ironic that at the time I was watching German parachutists falling from the skies over Heraklion, two years later I myself would be falling from airplanes. Anyway, I felt proud of myself, and at that moment, the light turned green. And with no hesitation I jumped out the door, feeling the airplane passing over me as I was going down at a great speed. I tried to keep my eyes open to enjoy the thrill of falling; but in no time, the parachute opened and, while I was swaying nicely, I was enjoying the view till I hit the ground. *I love it*, I said to myself. For sure, it was easier compared with the horror swing. I agreed now with that English Captain who refused to climb up to the swing!

The second jump was outside the airfield, and I was given the number two spot. On the plane, a young Englishman who was assigned number one asked me if I wanted to take his place—since he told me he was afraid he would freeze when the light turned green, and a small delay could be a disaster for the entire group. I said OK. I had done it before, and I did not mind to be first again and agreed. Just before we had reached the drop-off area, the sergeant walked up and saw that I was number one again. He came and told me to change positions and told me to push number one out the door if he showed some hesitation to jump when the light turned green!

The light turned green, and we jumped out, but I realized that my parachute was not opening on time as it had done so on the first jump, and I was going down like a bullet. They had told us that if the parachute did not open immediately, the air pressure would keep it closed, and we should pull the opposite straps apart to allow air to go in and open the parachute. So without losing time and hesitating, I did that and immediately the chute opened; and I felt that the straps would pull and separate my body apart from my armpits. A sergeant at the drop-off area, who was watching everybody falling, told me afterward that he thought that my parachute would not open and that I would have become another fatality in their parachute training area. "It was a good thing you did that, you pulled the ropes apart," he said to me.

The last days the drops would have to be from 750 feet and also from 500 feet.

Falling from 500 feet, you don't have time to look around you. If the chute didn't open in time, you'd die for sure.

"My god," I said. "On the 500-foot jumps, why do we drop from such a low height?" I thought the airplane was brushing the treetops just before we jumped out. Then the sergeant, who heard me saying that, said that since I was OSS, I should know that they would prepare me for a drop-off someplace in Greece. "If they drop you," he told me, "from two thousand feet and you take a couple minutes to fall down, Germans could be watching you and come quickly to capture you. But if they drop you from five hundred feet in an area where there are big trees and you fall between them and you hide, you would have a chance to survive. But of course," he said, "you should pray first of all that the chute opens on time and nobody spots you." Then I thought of the second jump when the chute didn't open, I said to myself that I was lucky the jump at that time was from two thousand feet; otherwise, if it was from five hundred feet, I would have been killed.

Our last jump was during the night. Though I used to like all the day jumps, the night jump was a very scary one, even to me who thought jumping from the airplanes was an exhilarating experience. Jumping in the night, especially in a dark night with no moon in the sky, is very scary. You jump out, you see nothing, and you pray the chute will open; and since you don't see the ground to prepare yourself, you just hit the ground hard. At the night drop, it was my bad luck that I fell on an area with bushes and thorns; and the pinlike thorns stuck all over me. Trying to free the parachute, which was entangled in the thorn bushes, was a very difficult job; and because I had been delayed in appearing at the pickup location, I heard the loudspeaker calling, "Number eight, where are you?" And finally a sergeant came with a big searchlight and helped me get out from that entanglement, and of course, his comment was, "Couldn't have found a better place to fall?"

Having finished our parachute training, the sergeant in charge thanked us for being such a good group and said that parachute jumping was a delightful experience and we should not be afraid if we had to utilize it. He told us that since he was jumping also with every group, he had jumped more than eight hundred times; and he said that he was so used to it that on the descent, he would unbuckle himself and hang with one hand before he'd land on the ground. It is sad to say this now, but four months after that day, just before I went on my mission, I heard that that sergeant was killed when his parachute did not open on a five-hundred-foot drop!

Having finished the parachute training, I was told that I was going to go to the English commando training camp nearby. We were told that it involved introduction to all light firearms and practice on them, plus various types of training in combatlike environment. There I fired all types of machine guns, and I even threw some grenades. I climbed ropes and ran over barricades and walls. It was lots of fun, and I liked it, except the firing of big guns. The noise was so deafening that I thought I had damaged my eardrums.

I was told that the camp was offering many aspects of commando training, and the one I was assigned to was for survival. Other training was more sophisticated given to real commandos who were supposed to invade or go someplace to destroy things. My training was more defensive, teaching me how to survive or defend myself in a difficult situation; and because of that, in about a week after I had been introduced to methods to defend myself, I was told that I would be sent to the radio operator's training outside of Haifa, Palestine. They mentioned to me that the rough training school for me was over and that the next phase would be easier and more interesting. With a car, they took me to that school, in the most beautiful area of Haifa. It was on top of a hill, and below was the harbor of Haifa. There were many rich homes on each side of a winding road that was connecting the harbor to the top of the hill in which the school was located. They took me inside the building that had many schoolrooms and introduced me to the English captain in charge. There I was supposed to start the training for wireless communication and learn to send and receive Morse code. The captain said that the Morse code class of about twenty people had started a week earlier, but I had missed it by going to the commando training. He hesitated to accept me since the other students were a week ahead of me, but he decided to put a special instructor for me in a different room, and he promised me that if I was able in just two days to learn what the others had learned in a week, then he would keep me.

Since I liked what I was doing, I learned all the letters the first day. In the second day, I told the instructor to increase the speed. He thought I was kidding, and he asked to see my notes. He told me that I was correct and he thought that I would not have any problem attending the big class on the third day. Truthfully enough, from the third day and on, not only was I following the progression in the big class, but I even passed the speed portion of receiving and sending Morse code, surprising even myself.

During the evenings, I was going to the Haifa nightclubs; and since I was the only American in the group, they expected me to pay for the drinks. I did not mind, though, since I was getting plenty of money. My monthly salary as a corporal T5 was $105, and since they were giving me $50 extra now for being a paratrooper, the total amount was $155. I was even making more than an English captain and tremendously more than an English or a Greek soldier who was getting $5 a month. That was the reason, and whenever we entered a nightclub, all the club girls would be after me for drinks. I realized though very late that I was spending too much money on those girls from whom I received just a couple of kisses.

After a couple of weeks of Morse code training, I was told that I had to return to Cairo where I would continue my spy training. I shook hands with the instructors, who were mostly English officers and with the two Greek classmates who supposedly were going to be sent to Greece by the English Intelligence Service. One of those Greeks was a captain and the other was a Cypriot with whom I had become very friendly with. As I squeezed their hands, I was wondering if we would ever meet again, or if any one of us three would survive.

Next morning, I and a few others left for Cairo; and after a full day's travel, we reached Cairo, the palace. Since I was absent for more than a month, I realized that some classmates were missing. The two Yugoslavians were gone; obviously, they were sent somewhere in Yugoslavia. I met with my brother, who was learning supervisory skills; obviously, they were planning some type of leadership position for him.

In actuality, he was sent to organize 6,500 partisans on Pelion Mountain near the big city of Volos, Greece. My brother, George, being the American agent and using American help and supplies, was utilizing the partisan's force for various sabotages and dynamiting of various German supply depots. His role was so effective that after the war he was decorated with the Legion of Merit.

A. *Instructions in the Art of Stealing*

Going back to the classroom with some old and some new classmates and new instructors, I was told that we were now going to have serious intelligence training. The instructor, who was a smiling lieutenant, said, "You should try to forget this particular lesson after your mission is over if you want to live a normal life and you don't want to find yourselves in prison or be rejected by society."

"In other words," he said, "the training you will receive to transform you into thieves, cheaters, and liars is for the purpose of doing only your job as a spy in order for you to enter certain premises to steal, photograph, or just read secret German documents or plans.

"As you all know," the lieutenant said, "suppose you are sent to a major enemy-held city. Your job would be to find out what they are planning so that you or others can stop them from doing it. Most of the time, you may never have a chance to get near the information, but suppose you had the chance but the information you were looking for was locked in some house or office; if you could only enter, you would love to steal the information crucial to us.

"Well, that is why we are going to teach you, how to open outside door locks and afterwards how to open drawer locks and safes. In other words, we will make all of you, gentlemen, thieves. You will circulate with civilians, but you will have the ability, when you have the chance, to steal the information that we need."

"So let's start with the outside door locks. For that, we will give you a set of master keys." And the lieutenant showed us a key chain with about two dozen sets of keys, and he explained, "Master keys are similar to these keys, for instance, the cleaning woman in a big hotel. She has a master key that opens all the hotel rooms, which might be twenty to one hundred rooms. With these master keys, you can probably open up to 70 percent of the door locks anywhere you would be going, and each one of you will get a set before you leave for your mission.

"Let's say, now, you have the master key," the lieutenant said, "and you have found the proper key and you open the door. Obviously, you would walk inside the room to find a locked drawer in which you suspect the information must be in. Should you get disappointed that what you are looking for is not on the table? You should know that no one leaves important documents out in the open, so we will teach you how to open drawers by using a tiny screwdriver, a thin wire, and a narrow metal plate."

For demonstration purposes, there were three tables with different locked drawers in the instruction room, and the lieutenant showed a different method that had to be used for each drawer in order to open them. After we had observed the lieutenant opening each drawer using these simple tools, we were each told to try following his directions. At the beginning, no one was successful, but as the lieutenant followed our hand movements and corrected them, of course, even we were surprised at how easy it was to open all three drawer locks.

When every student had opened all three table drawers and he saw the smiles of satisfaction on our faces, he smiled himself. And he told us that though it was easy to do it here, it would be more difficult under real conditions, which would involve time element and fear of being caught. He explained, "Under real conditions, when you have to open the drawer, take pictures and leave as quickly as possible. Our hands will not be as steady as they are now. They may tremble from fear, so if you had to open a drawer similar to the one you had just opened in only two trials, in the field, you will need four or five trials, or you may never be able to open it at all.

"So let us say that your hands were steady enough and you had opened the drawer and you found that the papers you were looking for are in the drawer, then you will try to take pictures, as quickly as possible, using the camera you will be provided. By the way, there will be a separate class on how to take pictures of documents. The Nikon camera you will be using, though it looks very small, costs a couple thousand dollars because it is made to take excellent pictures, even in very bad conditions. Just point and shoot, and you should be sure that even in the worst conditions, you will get what you are looking for.

"Let us say now," the lieutenant said, "that you had opened the drawer and that you had taken the pictures you wanted, do you leave a messy drawer and leave the room? No, no. The German plans and movements described in those documents you had just copied will be changed or be obsolete if the

Germans realized that someone had copied them. It is equally important that you put pages in order, the way you found them and lock the drawer before you leave. How we lock the drawer is a reverse process, which we should learn now with the same tools. Again, we will do the opposite movements we had done previously."

We all followed the lieutenant's hand movements, and real enough, all three open drawers were locked again. It did not take us much time, and we all did the same and proved to ourselves and to the lieutenant that we would be great thieves.

At that time, which was late afternoon, the chief, Major Vassos, came into the classroom. Obviously, he wanted to know from the lieutenant how well we were following the instructions, and from the smiling face of the lieutenant, we realized he was satisfied with our progress.

Before we were dismissed, the lieutenant, with a smile on his face, mentioned that the following day our training would be more challenging and we would be learning how to open safes, a training which would really give one a diploma for professional thievery.

The following day in the classroom, we saw one portable safe plus three combination lock units, which we guessed would be that day's instruction on how to open them.

"To open a safe," the lieutenant said, "you use no instruments or tools. You use your ear and your sense of feel. You must turn the knob right and then left and then right, and in these movements in order that the safe opens, a plunger must fall in a certain slot.

"The plunger will fall in if you know the combination and you stop at a certain number and you change direction. So if you turn the knob slowly and you reach the combination number, you should feel or sense a movement of the plunger, and that is exactly what we will be teaching you, to sense or feel a very slight movement of the plunger." We all watched the lieutenant open all the safes, and then our turn came to try. At the beginning, we could not sense anything, then he told us the combination number of one safe but he said to go to that number and don't turn in the opposite direction, just sense a slight movement of the plunger. We really did sense something, and we were glad for it. Then each one of us took another safe combination and slowly tried to sense their combination ourselves. It took us two days, but at the end of the second day, every one of us had opened all the safes. The lieutenant was extremely happy with our class's accomplishments, and he called the chief, Major Vassos, again to congratulate us, saying that our class's two-day accomplishment was very good compared to the three or four days that the other classes required to achieve what our class did in two days.

After openning these safes, we were told to be very careful in removing the documents. "It is very important to replace them in the same order we had found them. A messy replacement means someone had disturbed their order and would be necessary to delete them or change their execution.

"Try to take pictures of the important documents as quickly as possible, replace pages as you found them, close the door, and lock it by moving the knob a little, either direction. It is also very important to lock the room the safe was in, and if you have moved any furniture in getting to the safe, you should arrange the pieces of furniture as you found them before you leave the room.

"Again, a spy thief is a gentleman—a thief who does not take anything out. He only reads or copies the information he thinks are important, and he is so gentle in doing that that after he is finished, nothing is disturbed or altered.

"A spy thief," the lieutenant said, "should actually be a 'phantom thief' to be effective and useful in the organization.

Having finished teaching us how to open locks, drawers, and safes, thus completing the course in stealing, the lieutenant, pointed out that a good spy, besides being a thief, "should also be a cheater and a liar." For these instructions, he told us we would have another instructor who would take over, and we would be in a different classroom, equipped with movie projectors and various other equipment required for these instructions.

Since it was Friday afternoon, we were told that for our relaxation during the weekend, we could entertain ourselves by visiting the yacht docked a short distance from the palatial OSS school. The rear-deck area of the yacht was converted into many small cabins, which we could occupy during the weekend as we pleased.

We were also provided with our own bus to take us to Cairo. In Cairo we went often to the Grand Hotel. We were obliged to return to the school by using the school's bus, and nothing else. If we had missed the bus, we would call, and a special car would come to take us back to school. The reason, they said, was that there was a German spy ring in Cairo that was trying to get information and pictures of OSS agents, especially people and soldiers, staying at the palace school.

Because of that warning, and for our own protection, we followed their warnings and restrictions as we had been told.

B. *Instructions in the Art of Lying*

Having rested and entertained ourselves during the weekend by visiting either Cairo or the yacht on the Nile, we returned to the classroom; and we were introduced to a new instructor, who tried immediately to memorize our first names. Our real last names were not used for security reasons, so I was known only as Helias. My last name, Doundoulakis, was known only at HQ.

The instructor pointed out that his first lesson would be the importance of having the proper identification when we go on our mission. "As you all know, all of you are trained here to become agents, plainly called spies, who eventually will be sent to a certain area or city and stay there for a specified period of time living with the people there, pretending to be part of their community. Because of that, you are supposed to have the proper identification, similar to what everyone living in that area is supposed to have. Your first name will stay as it is, but your last name would be any common name you would prefer." He asked us if we had chosen a name, and since almost all the others gave him their preferred last name, instantly a name came to my mind, which to me was very common and easy to remember, and I said, "I would like my last name to be Nikolaou." He wrote it down, and he told me that my fake identification would show my name to be Helias Nikolaou. "The address you are supposed to live in will be picked up from the telephone book of the town or city you will be sent to."

The instructor emphasized that the identification we would be given was temporary, just to have some identification during our travel toward our final goal. "Once you established residence, you will need to find a way to get a permanent place. The purpose of the temporary card with the fake address is to have some identification to show the Gestapo in case we get caught in a sudden police or Gestapo street search.

"Let us say now," the lieutenant said, "that you reached your final destination and you get a place to stay, you should go and find the address your temporary identification indicates. If that address is within a residential neighborhood, you should not rush to replace your card. But if the address happens to be a store, a hotel, or even a museum, then it is vitally important to replace your card with the correct address, not because of the Gestapo, who will not recognize if your address is legitimate or not, but because of the Greek police who can distinguish immediately if the address you use is residential or not. If you were taken to that city with someone who knew the city before, then you probably have a place to stay temporarily till you find or rent a suitable place to establish as residence. Having a place to stay, your next responsibility would be to find a suitable place to install your wireless. Don't use your residence as the place for the wireless. Since the place where you will operate your wireless should be guarded or visited by a few people every day, you should engage in some type of business in order to justify the presence of a few people in that place every day. Try to find and rent a big store or warehouse and pretend to sell something in that location so the neighbors won't mind the presence of a few people every day. Don't forget that you will have to install an antenna at least fifty to seventy feet long with a direction toward the south or toward Cairo.

"Another reason you should not operate your wireless where you reside is so you will have a place to stay in case they find your radio and you have escaped capture.

"But if the Gestapo knows both addresses—that is, the place you reside and the place where you operate your wireless, then you should have a secure third address to go to in case the Gestapo is looking for you.

"Let us say," the lieutenant said, "that the Gestapo followed you for a few days and knows where you reside and at the end, finds the location where you operate your radio and raids the place but you were lucky and you escape. Where would you go and make contact with the organization if you had not made any prior arrangements?

"If you're chased by the Gestapo, you cannot go and stay in hotels or run around the streets. The safest step would be to hide in some friendly house till you are able to be evacuated from that city. So right from the start, you should have established three addresses for your use. One for your living quarters, one for establishing and operating the wireless, and a third one for hiding and contacting members of the organization.

"Up to this lesson," the lieutenant said, "we taught you how to proceed and establish a communication center from the city you will be sent to, and the OSS headquarters in the Middle East. Having established your three places to reside or operate now, we analyze the place where you will operate your radio. Having placed your antenna in such a way that it is not visible to any visitor that comes in the room, you should have its end accessible at the place you have chosen to sit and operate your radio, but at the same time, the end of the antenna should be hidden smartly, as you choose. Arrange some books on the table or desk to help you hide the radio. A table should always be there on which to place the radio and a few guns or grenades easily accessible to be used in case of a sudden Gestapo raid. You should establish a hiding place for the radio, battery, guns, grenades, working pads, and any other items you think would expose your secret underground operation.

"Your radio operating location should be converted in such a way that in a critical moment of a Gestapo raid, you will have access to a planned escape route. The best way to try to escape would be to try to jump to the adjoining house and escape from that home's roof or yard.

"At the time you are sending a message," the lieutenant said, "you should know you are exposed to all the radio receivers including the Gestapo's triangulation instruments, so you must send your message as fast as you can and get off the air. Receiving messages is no problem, but at the time you are sending, if a triangulation receiver hears you, the operator of that instrument can immediately locate the direction of your signals. If they realize that you are very close to them, they install a few other triangulation instruments in various other locations. And they can locate the region of your signal. If your signal is very strong, they immediately know you are very close to them. They also know how many wirelesses of their own are operating in your own area, so if they decide to locate you, they restrict the activity of their own radios in order to concentrate easier on you and locate you. For that reason, try to send only one message, maximum two messages, if they are short, and not more than twenty-five words for each message. The maximum time to send messages and be on air should not be more than five minutes. If you want to send another urgent message, you should change frequency and tell the receivers of your message which frequency you want to switch to. Generally, the best policy is to change frequency for every additional message you want to send.

"While you are sending "telegrams" or messages," the lieutenant said, "you should have at least two people guarding you. One should walk around the block where you are operating the wireless, must be very alert and devoted to your safety, and be willing to run and notify you of any Gestapo raid even if he is endangered of being caught himself. The second guard should be in or outside the house where you are working and should watch every person entering the premises and, if necessary, should be ready to fight and be willing to kill anyone who enters the room where you are operating the wireless. In case a stranger sees you with headphones on and your activities are exposed to strangers, immediately everyone in that facility, including yourself, should vacate the area and hide elsewhere and expect the worst, that the stranger might tell others. And that the Gestapo might soon invade the premises.

"As I said, to account for your daily presence and that of some other persons at the premises where you operate the wireless, it is recommended that you pretend you are engaged in some type of business," the lieutenant said. "The easier and most commonly used front is to be merchants, pretending to sell certain items wholesale. You don't want people to enter your store all day long. You will pretend that you provide other smaller stores of those items you are selling, and generally, your selling prices would be higher than ordinary so that not too many shoppers, perhaps no one, would be interested in buying your items.

"It will be, of course, a very unorthodox type of business to try to sell at a higher price, that you have no customers," said the lieutenant with a smile on his face. "But being a spy means doing many things contrary to the ordinary.

"To summarize what we have covered up to this point," the instructor said, "you have gone to your destination, you have found and established the three residences, you have opened a business, you have made contact with OSS headquarters in Cairo, and you thought everything was going OK until one day the Germans looking for partisans have caught many people and you are among those people. The Germans examine everyone, and your turn comes to be examined. You show them where you live, and they ask you what you were doing in the city you're now living in. Of course, you should not tell them that you have a business somewhere there since you should never expose the place where you hide and operate the wireless. At this point, since you are young and you could very easily be a student, find out what universities or trade or business schools are operating in that city and go and find out what programs are starting in the near future and inquire or register for those courses. A registration document would be a perfect justification for living in that city in which case you don't need to have parents or relatives to be living there. This, of course, is if you were caught and detained at random, and is not related to the organization. If you were caught, however, and suspected to be a member of our organization, that case is more serious; and for that, you will learn how to fabricate false stories. You have to be careful, though," the instructor said, "not to show that you are scared, and do not tremble. No matter how innocent you are, if you show you are scared and your hands are trembling, the Gestapo, who is trained to analyze suspects, will think that you are hiding something and will not believe your story. Unless you are caught with your headphones on your ears, you have a chance to deny everything. So when someone asks you a question, immediately remind yourself to be calm and with a sure sign of confidence, tell them what first comes to your mind. Even if the story is stupid or completely wrong, the way you say it will weigh more than the story. In other words, in these situations on which your life depends, you must train yourself to become a great liar. It is an art in life for someone to be a good liar. Some of the world's most successful businessmen were great liars. They succeeded in life by convincing other influential people to trust them, to help them in many financial situations, and they formed corporations, planned by people with ideas and dreams."

He said that to be a good liar is an art and many times has a purpose. It could save somebody else's life, but in our instruction as a spy, it is a very important asset and could very well save your own life.

The instructor emphasized that the instructions up to now were showing us how to camouflage ourselves while living with civilians. "The following

To demonstrate the importance of lying and fabricating a story, I will demonstrate now how I was saved from being caught by fabricating an effective story at the proper time! After I had finished five months of spying training in Cairo, Egypt, I was sent to the second city of Greece, Salonica, a very strategically located city.

I went without being caught for nine months. I had established a wireless cell in that city, sending valuable messages daily and causing great damage to the enemy.

However, one summer day, after having sent a couple of telegrams to Cairo, I went for a swim at a public swimming pool in Salonica. Either I forgot to take my watch off my wrist or I was afraid that it would be stolen, so I went swimming with it. After I came out of the water and was going to my lounge chair, two men, sunning themselves nearby called me and asked to see my watch, which happened to be a very sophisticated and accurate American-made watch given to me in Cairo to be used for my underground service. Immediately, I realized that I had made a mistake of wearing this watch while swimming, violating the rules I had been taught; but at this particular moment, I had to act quickly to get away from this predicament, and undo my mistake.

The two men, who happened to be German officers, looked at the watch and asked me where I got it. I immediately thought of what we had learned in Cairo on how to resolve unexpected difficult situations by remaining calm as though nothing was happening and to try to fabricate a story that would make sense. I had been asked where I got the watch—a watch that was American-made, very accurate, and expensive. Many years had passed since then, and I still wonder and ask myself how I thought so fast and had given such a logical answer that even the Germans had to accept it as true. Without hesitation, I told the Germans that I had bought it from a fellow German soldier by giving him fresh eggs, nuts, and some money. The German soldier could have gotten it from a dead American soldier, and since he had other watches, he wanted to sell this one. The Germans heard the fabrication, looked at each other, and then looked at me. They believed me and gave me my watch back. After all, in front of them was an innocent-looking nineteen-to-twenty-year-old young man, how could they ever think that this innocent-looking young man was a corporal in the U.S. army and a spy in the OSS? I got my watch and walked away, blaming myself for my stupidity in wearing my watch while swimming, but also, I congratulated and thanked myself for fabricating such a convincing answer that even the German officers had to accept it. It was a proof to me that the five months of training was worth it and more, and that I should follow more carefully what I had been taught.

instructions," the lieutenant said, "will be in situations that are more involved, and you will have to find ways to get out or escape. Let us take the case where you are, let us say, in a restricted area by an airfield, counting the German airplanes when you are caught by a patrol unit and you are questioned to justify your presence in a restricted area. Since most of you are very young, you might say that you went the wrong way and you got lost. If you don't carry any suspicious items or arms, even if you are searched, you will have a great chance of being released. That is why you should not try to make notes even if the items you wanted to remember are many. Let us say you want to remember the number of airplanes that you observed in an airfield before a scheduled sabotage. You counted twelve small airplanes at field A, you also counted eight big-troop transport airplanes in field B, and around two hundred barrels of gas in field C. This information is very valuable, and you would like to write them down on a piece of paper. If you did and you were caught, you would not have a chance to prove you were innocent. Since there is a big chance to be caught before you get out from that forbidden area, try to memorize what you saw. Don't make notes. Also, never enter a restricted area with a concealed camera. Being caught with a camera is a proof that you wanted to take pictures, and until the pictures in the camera are developed, you will be kept and guarded.

"Let us say now that you made the mistake and you wrote down on a piece of paper the information on the airplanes described above. Or even if you did not have anything on you but the guard wanted to take you in for questioning. And you knew that the investigation would find something against you and you would rather prefer to avoid that interrogation if it is only one German guard. You should utilize the pen gun to kill the German. Before you leave for your mission, you will be provided a pen gun, which you will have in your pocket, and though it could be used to write with, it can also be used to kill in special situations. This pen gun will have only one bullet so it could be useful in situations where there is only one German to kill in an isolated area, where no other Germans are around.

"If in a situation where the German guard pushes you to proceed toward the guard station where there would be a thorough examination, you pretend you want to write a name and you take your pen gun out, point it toward the guard's heart, and press the back of the pen. A small bullet would come out from the pen gun, and if you are only a couple of feet from the German, the German would be killed. Even if you wounded the German, you would still have a good chance to escape in the confusion.

"But let us say there were two Germans instead of one, and they're taking you to the guard station or to their interrogation center. They tell you to wait for their examiner to come. They lock the door, and since they don't really know you are a spy, they don't guard you too strictly. Your obligation would be to find a way to escape before the examiner comes. There are many ways for someone to escape if he is alone. One is by breaking the door, another is by jumping from a window or putting on someone else's clothes and walking out. If a guard is left to watch, you use the pen gun to kill him or find a killing instrument with which to attack him. We will teach you how you can make a sharp killing instrument by tightly folding a plain newspaper."

At this point, the lieutenant brought up half a dozen hardcover, four-page colored books similar to the early-age children's books, each book specifying different room conditions, and explained to us that by studying each room or house situation or provisions, we should be able to invent a way to escape. He went through each book, describing the provisions of each room or house, and then he was asking us to invent an escape route. In one case, for example, there could be a tree leaning on the wall where a window was near, and it would be easy to use the tree to get down and try to escape, and in another there was a toolbox with many tools with which the lock or the door could be opened. In one picture, there was a German soldier's overcoat and a hat, in which case they expected us to put it on, jump from the window and get out right by the German guards at the gate.

It is important to note that for each book in which there was a different way to escape, the lieutenant, while everybody was listening, was concentrating his questions and attention mostly on one of us, one at a time. And we noticed that after each book was analyzed and its escape route was finally defined, he was putting notes in his book as if he was grading each one of us on our way of thinking and our intelligence ability in inventing escape routes. We had noticed that he was marking us on many occasions, especially if one of us came up with an original plan. We used to ask ourselves why we were getting marked on our performance or fast response. Did that mean that we had to pass a certain grade to be considered spy material and finally graduate? Would one of us fail, not be dependable spies and be rejected from our assignment? We said to ourselves that though they needed us, if we had failed to get a passing mark, in the interest of the organization and also for us, they would rather prefer to lose a prospective agent than send someone whom they had determined would be unable to go through those unrealistic self-sacrificing situations day after day. Thinking those thoughts among ourselves pushed us to try harder to prove our capabilities and to start paying more attention in class and to try as much as we could to explore every discussed situation as if it was a real situation on which our life depended, and thus must be resolved. It was interesting to note now that in the following weeks, we found out that the marks had a lot to do with our assignments; the students with the highest performance were going to be sent to the more dangerous missions.

As the lieutenant continued his lecture of critical conditions in which we would have to escape in order to save our lives, he tried hard to emphasize to us how crucial it would be to find a way to escape. If we were found carrying secret documents or some type of arms, those items would be sufficient proof against us; and we should expect extensive interrogation to follow. He did not want to discuss the various methods the Gestapo usually used to force enemy agents to talk, which would make us scared thinking about the consequences; but we did not have to be told about it. We had heard of such torturing Gestapo episodes in which fingers were crushed and electric shocks were utilized in order to coerce agents to talk, forcing them to give-in; where they had come from, what their job was, and who were their associates, and other questions. In general, individuals who had been proven to be enemy agents would rather terminate themselves with the poison Q pills that they had hidden on them rather than die by torture. If we were guarded by a single guard, we should try to find a favorable opportunity to fight with him, get his gun, and kill him. It was pointed out that if that try also failed and the German guard killed us instead, death would be more preferable than dying through torture. At least we tried and died heroically. Coming to the end of the instructions of how to live as a spy in normal and also in abnormal conditions, the instructor at the end, in order to encourage us, pointed out that the life of a spy was the most fascinating; and it would be the life to brag about to our kids and friends in the future if we made it. "You will be," he told us, "the true actors of fascinating true movies of the war." He also told us that his dream was, to be sent to Greece, but as he pointed out, his Greek American accent did not permit him. "I envy all of you," he told us, "for being a spy in SI, living in a strange city with unknown civilians and Germans. I wish I could go, it would have been a once in a lifetime experience.

The "Q" pill was a small glass vial filled with enough cyanide for a "quick" death.

"I may be sent," he said, "as a member of another category, maybe in the saboteur category and it may be more dangerous than what you will go through. But to be a spy in category SI is something special. It would be an experience worth participating under any circumstance."

Before coming to the end of his lecture, the instructor also mentioned a few things for us to remember.

Living with civilians who may include people working with the German Gestapo, would mean that we must be careful of the following:

1. Don't ask questions you should know the answers to, or questions that everyone should know the answer to, as this would indicate that you are not from that area.
2. At dinner, use both hands if the others do that.
3. When buying things or paying for services, know what amount they are asking.
4. Find out the transportation in your area; if other people use buses or trains or taxis to go to various locations, use the same.
5. Find out where you can buy things like stamps, where the restaurants are, the banks, and other local places.
6. Don't have a steady girlfriend, and don't take your date to expensive restaurants and stores. Her previous boyfriend will get jealous of you, and he could be worse than the Gestapo.
7. Don't spend money excessively in a country where people are dying from hunger.
8. Most importantly, you will go to the country you are going with a great spirit to do the job you're required to do, and with great faith, you will come back and talk about it.

Good luck and a safe return!

The following sessions were devoted to test me for my Morse code ability and teach me a few things about the wireless mechanism.

A testing proved that I was able to receive at least twenty words, each word of five letters per minute. The extensive Morse code training in Cairo and also in Palestine proved sufficient enough.

Now I had to learn how to cipher or to code the message before sending it. I had to use a method to do that. I was given a phrase to memorize, and by substituting those letters, our telegram would be coded. The entire coding process depended on that phrase. For a few hours, we practiced how to code and decode telegrams; and finally, he told us that we should memorize that phrase and burn the paper after we were sure we would not forget it in the following weeks or months from now. "Don't forget," he told us, "your mission will be worthless if at the time you want to use it to send the messages, you forget your phrase in order to code your messages. An uncoded message cannot be sent, so be sure you memorize it well before you burn it." The more I had tried to keep it in my mind, the more I was missing a letter or a word. I was singing it or relating it to a story, so at the end of the day, I was very sure I would not forget; so I decided to burn it and swore to myself that I would not forget that phrase ever.

We were also getting an overall lesson of the type of wireless we would be using and how to do simple repairs, how to attach the battery, and how the wireless should be handled.

Since we knew that most of us would be dropped by parachute to the chosen location and since the wireless would be dropped together with us, our responsibility would be, after reaching the ground, to pick up the radio, hoping it was in an accessible spot. We had been assured that if the radio had to be dropped by parachute, the radio would be in a shockproof container, and would no doubt be in good condition. Of course, small connections would have to be done at the place of operation, which we had been trained for.

Chapter 6

- Assignment to a secret and dangerous mission and preparation to be dropped by parachute outside from the city of Salonica, Greece
- Plans changed to be sent by boat to Greece, rather the by parachute.
- Buying civilian clothes with no markings.
- Was given a nylon belt to wear, which had sewed in its linings 150 gold sovereigns. Was issued a .32 caliber pistol.

Having finished all lessons and having not been rejected up to that point, I was finally told that I had to report to the office of the chief, Major John Vassos. I said to myself, *Is his invitation good news? Am I ready to go? Have I proven that I could undertake any type of dangerous assignments?* I would be very disappointed if I had been rejected, but while I was putting those ideas in my mind, I realized that it must be good news because as I was going to his office, I saw that the major was waiting outside and with open hands, he embraced me and congratulated me saying, "Bravo, Helias, you are ready, and you are on the top of the list!" Obviously, the marks given to me by the instructors were quite high, but another thought came to mind; the higher the mark, the more dangerous the mission!

Major Vassos told me to sit down, and then he told me that I was ready to go and that they had two very interesting missions for me. One would be to go with Captain James Kelly, the officer who had come to the Iliopolis Villa where the English were housing us and took us to the OSS, and I would be dropped by parachute on the partisan-held Greek mountaintops to get information of their ammunition needs. For the other mission, I would be dropped outside of Salonica (or Thessaloniki), the second largest city in Greece, and form an underground organization with a Greek officer who knew Salonica well; and I would have to stay in Salonica till the end of the war. He emphasized to me that the Salonica mission, though more attractive, would be more dangerous since Salonica was the center of German troop movements and was guarded more than any other city, including Athens, but it was up to me to choose.

Thinking that I would be unlucky enough to jump and break a leg, even though I loved to jump from airplanes, I told him I would prefer the Salonica mission. "To tell you the truth," Major Vassos said, "I think you're better fit for that mission." You are good, young, and have no accent, so though Captain James Kelly was hoping to get you as his wireless operator, I want to warn you, it would be more dangerous in Salonica. Be careful when you are on the air, don't stay too long on the air. The Gestapo will be listening.

"Since you chose the Salonica mission and we need you to leave as quickly as possible, the sergeant in the next office will give you a belt with 150 English sovereigns and money to go and buy civilian clothes, underwear, and shoes. But be careful that the tailor's marks don't disclose where they were bought." He warned me not to tell anyone where I was going, wished me good luck and a safe return. Next door the sergeant showed me the nylon belt with many small pockets around it, which was filled up with 150 sovereigns, and at the right side, the belt had a bigger pocket. The sergeant told me I could put a small .32 caliber gun in it if I wanted to take it. I told him I would rather not take the gun, since if I had to go through checkpoints, the belt with the gold could hide under my clothes, but the gun could protrude and be shown.

"I cannot force you to take the gun," the sergeant said. "But why not take it and, if you're supposed to go through checkpoints, throw it out before you reach the point of checking? On the other hand, suppose you have no gun and you get examined and they find your belt and the gold, would you rather have a gun at that point to try to escape than have nothing at all? You're not guilty enough with the 150 gold sovereigns!" After listening to him, I agreed with the sergeant and took the gun. Also, I was given the pen gun. The following day, with the Egyptian money I had been given, I went shopping; but I had difficulty finding clothes without labels. All suits in Cairo were made to order, that is, you couldn't buy a suit off the rack. So, the tailor placed his labels all over the suit. I tried not to offend him, but I told him to remove the labels, which he did, for a little more money. When

I told him I wanted to pick it up in two days, the tailor said, "What is the big hurry?" I had to pay him more to have it finished on time. In a couple of days, I was told to be ready to be taken to the airport OSS mission center where a parachute would be given to me and directions of my drop and also in getting a radio.

To my surprise, I was told that a message had come from the Salonica area that wherever I would be dropped, outside of Salonica, I would be caught. There was high German troop concentration in that area and it would be a miracle for a parachute not to be spotted. I would most certainly be caught. They suggested the agent be brought in by boat, someplace far away from the city, and as soon as possible, since valuable information of German movements was needed. I was notified immediately of the change in plans, and instead of going to the airport, I was told that I would make my way to Salonica by boat, first going to neutral Turkey, to Izmir, a city along the coast.

Chapter 7

- Trip by boat from Alexandria, Egypt, to Cyprus, to Izmir, Turkey, then to an American base north of Izmir
- First attempt to go to Greece failed due to rough seas.
- Second attempt successful, leaving three spies on a deserted part of the Halkidiki Peninsula called Kassandra, fifty miles south of Salonica.

Since the proper boat to be used for our mission was in Alexandria, I was taken in an OSS car to Alexandria, and in the harbor of Alexandria, we located the boat. The boat was originally a Greek fishing boat over forty-five feet long, but the OSS hired the boat and the crew in Turkey. They put two tank engines in the boat so we were told, and made this boat very fast.

Inside, I met a Greek officer named Spyros who had been recruited by the OSS and who had the same belt around him, and who was going to another city in northern Macedonia, called Edessa.

Also, there was an American soldier who was going to be left at the OSS office in Izmir, Turkey.

After the boat left, the captain told us that in order to go to Turkey, we would have to go through Cyprus. Besides the captain, there were two Greek sailors. The captain told us the story of how they happened to be recruited by the OSS, and he said that the boat was in Greece but had been taken by the Germans and that the Germans forced them into serving the Germans' needs and giving them only food in return. One day the three Greeks attacked the Germans with knives and killed them, and took the boat to Turkey where they joined the OSS. I heard one of the Greek sailors say that we, the

Americans, must have lots of money with us, and that if they killed us, they would be rich. The captain heard him and told him that he did not know who was the real enemy and who was not, and if he heard him again saying such stupid things, he would throw him into the sea. Anyway, I warned the other two passengers to be careful and not stray far from the group, that we should stick together.

We reached Cyprus the following morning, and after we got needed provisions, we left for Turkey when we realized that the sailor we did not like had been substituted by a very polite man and a good fisherman. Since then, we were supposed to travel only at daytime and make port in Turkish coastal villages at night. This fisherman showed me how to catch fish using a strong light and a fork attached to the end of a stick to spear the fish. Traveling, we had two flags, displaying each one accordingly as needed, using the Turkish flag if we saw a German patrol boat and using the Greek flag if we saw a Turkish patrol boat.

Passing through the narrows between the Greek island of Samos and the Turkish mainland, where the distance was less than a mile, the captain warned us that we would be traveling dangerously, since the Germans had an observation post on the island of Samos, and since we would be displaying a Turkish flag, the Turks would have to search the boat prior to collecting the toll for passing through this restricted area. "If we don't stop," the captain said, "they may chase after us or fire at us in which case the Germans may get suspicious and chase after us too."

As per our captain's instructions, we smiled at the Turks and waved at them, pretending that we were slowing down to stop. Having passed by the station, he told us, to "fall down," and put the boat into full throttle, and got us away. Fortunately, the Turks did not feel like chasing a small Turkish fishing boat, since we were flying the Turkish flag, and never fired or chased after us. As the captain said, "we were just lucky that time!"

After that incident, the captain told us that the next stop would be Smyrna, or Izmir as the Turks called it. In Izmir we were told not to walk outside since there were many German spies taking pictures of the newcomers, knowing full well that Americans sent spies from there to other Greek cities. In Smyrna I was called to the OSS office where I was given an envelope that contained thousands of Greek drachmae, or Greek money.

Also, since I had to have a Greek identification, I was asked what I would like to use as a surname. "Any name," the sergeant said, "except your real last name." I told him I had chosen the name Nikolaou while training, and that I should use the same name now, which happened to be a very commonly used Greek name. They also took my picture, and until the identification papers were ready, the sergeant brought me a can of oil, and he told me, "Here is a present for you. Be careful with it, and since it is very heavy, don't drop it. It is your radio at the bottom of the container; and above the radio, in another compartment, is olive oil.

"Also," the sergeant said, "until we have prepared your identification, I will introduce you to the person with whom you will be working." In the next room, I met a man about forty years old named Cosmas Yiapitzoglou, who came to me, embraced me, and told me he was anxious to meet me. He also mentioned he was proud to know that the American OSS trusted him so much that they gave him an American soldier as a wireless operator. He told me he had spent many years in Salonica, and he knew hundreds of friends who would provide us information.

Then he saw the can of oil and asked me, "What is that?" I said it was a can of olive oil, a present for us. "What," he said, "we don't need olive oil, we will be eating in the best restaurants. Leave it here. We have other more important items to carry!" I smiled, and I told him that in the bottom of the can was the radio I will be using. "Really," he said. "Very smart idea. Who would ever think a radio is hidden in that container?" At that moment, the Greek officer who came with me from Alexandria and who was going to Edessa and whose name was Spyros, walked in, holding the same type of oilcan with him. When Yiapitzoglou saw him holding the same can, he told me, "Is he also going to prepare food?"

"Yes," I said. "As a matter of fact, he will be with us on the same boat and he is to be dropped on the same Greek shore in the next couple of days."

After getting my identification, the captain told us to get to the boat, and he told us that before we arrived at the final American base near the island of Mitilini, we would stop overnight in a small harbor. The captain knew that harbor, which was between two hills, and it would offer a calm sea for us to pass the night. The trip from Smyrna to that harbor was very rough, but when we reached the harbor, the sea was very calm and peaceful. The captain said that in this spot a Greek cruiser named *Andreas* hit a German mine two years ago and sank, and twenty-one sailors drowned.

At the end of the harbor, we saw a fishing boat, the size of ours, filled with so many women, children and old men that there was no room to sit, and all were standing and crying. We were told that those people were refugees, chased away by the Germans from the island of Rhodes and hoping to be accepted by the Turks. The Turks had stopped accepting any more refugees since they had to feed them, and the captain of that boat was thinking to sink the boat in that harbor in order for the Turks to accept the refugees. In the meantime, the Turkish guards were watching and did not allow the boat to sink. As we found out, the people had not eaten anything for two days; and they were in a pitiful, desperate state. While I was watching the people crying, a baby less than one year old apparently died in the hands of his mother who was screaming, holding the dead baby. The captain of that boat immediately picked up the baby and, holding it by the feet upside down, dipped the baby in and out of the cold water. The baby revived, vomited enough which, as we found out, were dried figs. The mother said that for two days, since she had not eaten anything, she had no milk in her breasts to feed her baby; and she was feeding him dried figs. The baby revived but was crying continuously. I could not bear looking at them in that situation, so I went to our captain and asked him if I could take a box of cookies, cans of milk, and other food to give to these desperate people. At the beginning, he hesitated; but afterward, he said that he was working for the Americans, and since, we, the Americans wanted them, why not! I filled up a big box of milk with other food items, and when the people saw me giving them food, everyone stretched out their hands to get something. First I gave two cans of milk for the baby and food to the mother. I went back and brought another carton of food, and all were thanking me. And one old woman said, "Thank you, my boy, God bless you and let God protect you wherever you go." I replied to her that I wished God would help them and find a safe place for them. As I was leaving to go to our boat, I looked at the baby who had calmed down; and he was finishing the last drop of the milk I had given his mother.

The next day in the afternoon, we reached the American base across from the island of Mitilini, the last stop before leaving for Greece. The base was in a remote area, and you could see only Turkish guards patrolling the area. It was the Thursday before Greek Easter, the beginning of April, 1944. The captain told us we should rest because the following evening we should leave for Greece. At that moment, we heard people coming from the woods, and we saw three young Turks pulling a small wild pig they had killed. Since the Turks were not allowed to eat pig's meat, they wanted to sell it to us, knowing we were Greeks and they knew that Greeks liked pig's meat. *It is not a bad idea,* I said to myself. *The pig seems to be a young pig and would make delicious chops, but who would skin it?* The boys agreed to get ten dollars for the pig and another ten dollars to skin it and cut the meat ready for cooking. I gave them the money, and they hung the pig in an adjoining tree to do the skinning. Yiapitzoglou and Spyros came out, and they were very glad to hear of my planned feast with pig's meat that evening and also the following day before we left for Greece. The following day, we realized that the weather was getting bad and that the sea was very rough. The captain was very skeptical of leaving, but he said that he had seen worse weather and he had no problem controlling the boat. As we worried about the weather, we again heard a lot of squeeling; and we saw four other boys pulling another wild pig, bringing it to us. Obviously, word went around that we had bought a wild pig the previous day; and these other four boys went and killed this one, which was four times bigger than the one we had bought the previous day. We told them that we were ready to leave and that we still had meat left from the previous one, but they did not want to listen, they were begging us to buy it. One said that the boar almost killed him because, after he had wounded the boar, it went after him and attacked him; and if the other three boys had not gone with knives to kill the boar, the boar would have killed the boy. I felt sorry for them, and I told them that I would give them $10 for the boar and another $10 to dig a hole and bury it. They agreed, and they started digging the hole away from the base.

Before it got dark, the captain told us to put all our belongings in the boat because he had decided to leave despite the bad weather. The two sailors loaded the boat with many supplies to be left in Greece—bags of rice, canned food, guns, and ammunition. When I went inside the boat, I saw that the space in the area in the rear of the boat was taken up by big bags and boxes; so I went to the front of the boat, and I saw a porthole where they kept the ropes. I sat outside, hanging my feet inside the porthole. At the start of the journey, the waves were not that big; but when the boat got farther from the harbor, the waves went over the front part of the boat, and the water was going over the hole and my head. Unable to go back where the others were, being afraid of falling overboard, I knelt inside the porthole and pulled down the cover of the porthole. By the time I got the cover on, one wave was coming after the other. And the compartment I was in filled halfway with water, and I knelt inside, holding tightly to the cover as the waves seemed to be passing over the top of the entire boat. The waves must have been so big that sometimes it looked to me that the boat was going straight up to heaven, and in a couple of seconds, it was plummeting down to hell. Though I seldom got seasick, that time I could not help myself; it looked as if I was in a wild roller-coaster ride. I could not help myself, and I vomited. I thought of my mother at that time who must have been in church for Good Friday service, singing the sad Byzantine hymns of Christ's death. If she only knew in what terrible condition I was in, ready to be drowned, she would have called the priest to pray for me. Being tossed up and down for more than two hours, I felt sorry for not being able to have been dropped by parachute as it was planned, even if that way of going to Salonica was more dangerous in being caught. At least people would know what happened to me rather than vanish at the bottom of the Aegean Sea. Kneeling, the vomit floated around me, and I accepted my death. All of a sudden, there was no more up-and-down movement. A chill came over my cheeks, and I said to myself, *We are sinking.* Instantly, I pulled the porthole cover tighter as if I wanted to prevent the water from coming in, maybe we were going down and have not reached the bottom of the ocean yet. *But then*, I thought, *suppose the ocean is a thousand feet deep, how would that help? If I plan to get out, let me open the cover and see if water is coming in.* As I moved the cover, to my surprise, no water was coming in; and immediately, I tried to stick my head out and look for the others. I tried to get out from the porthole, but having knelt for five hours, I had difficulty doing so. When I finally got out, the others saw me; and I heard one hollering, "Helias is alive. He has not fallen out." I walked toward them as they all stared at me as if I had come from hell; some were laughing at me because I looked so dirty and wet. They thought I had fallen in the water during the night. I looked at them with a mad expression, complaining why nobody came to look for me, why nobody cared! Nobody missed me? They said that they saw me at the beginning standing in that porthole, but afterward when I got in and covered myself with the porthole cover, the waves were so big nobody thought I would be in that hole. They thought the waves had knocked me over. Yiapitzoglou said that he was glad to see me and told me to go and change before I caught cold. At that point, I asked if we had reached Greece. I was told that we had returned almost near the area we had started from. Yiapitzoglou said that because of the bad weather, the boat could not go fast and would not reach our destination before daybreak and it would be dangerous to travel during daytime. Also, he told the captain to return because he didn't know what he would do in Salonica without a radio operator, thinking that I had drowned. Coming back, he would have asked for another radio operator. "Anyway, I am very glad that I don't have to look for another radio operator. I like you very much, and I think we will make a very good team," Yiapitzoglou said. Half heatedly, I said "Thank you."

It was Saturday, the day before Easter, and the captain told us that we should rest that day and the following day. "Easter day in the afternoon, we will leave for Greece, praying for calm seas. To tell you the truth," the captain said, "I was never more scared than last night. I did not want to say anything to the others, but, I thought I would not be able to control the boat and would capsize. We must have had over ten Beauforts of rough weather."

The following morning, Easter day, the sun was bright; and the sea seemed much calmer. Turkish soldiers came to us as we were eating breakfast, and knowing that it was Easter that day, they offered to bring us goat's meat in exchange for aspirin and canned food. We agreed, and with the meat they brought us, we cooked many chops, which was a way to celebrate Easter; and we thanked God that we had not drowned the previous night.

In the early afternoon, the captain told us to go to the ship; and jokingly, he turned to me and said that he did not expect to see me going to that porthole again. He said that many sacks of rice had gotten wet and were taken out from the boat, so there would be plenty of room in the back for everyone. Since the weather seemed to be OK, we should arrive at the tip of Halkidiki around four o'clock just before daybreak.

We left Turkey's shores, and in about an hour, we passed near a very small island on which there was a tall lighthouse. One family was put there by the Germans to take care of the lighthouse. Once a week, the Germans would bring food to that family comprised of the husband, his wife, and their two little children. As soon as they saw us, they waved to us and told us to stop and tell them how the war was going. They had no radio, nobody to talk to or any newspaper to read to find out or to learn what was happening. They passed their lonely hours fishing all day long. We gave them some rice and cookies for their kids and then left.

Beaufort is a measure of rough seas. A number three is a typical condition.

Chapter 8

- Arrival on the Greek shore at the tip of the Kassandra peninsula at 4:00 AM
- American OSS agent travels on a German boat, manned by German sailors, while wearing belt with 150 gold sovereigns and a .32 calibergun
- Safe arrival of can of olive oil with wireless in the hidden compartment

Leaving that island, we knew we were in German-occupied Greece. At any time, we might see a German patrol boat coming from any island, in which case a Turkish flag would not help. After three hours of uneasy travel, the captain installed mufflers on the exhaust of the engines. He told us not to talk loud since the sound traveled far, especially in calm seas. At that time, maybe after the storm or after our prayers, the sea had calmed down so much that it looked as if it was a lake. The only thing you heard was a mild puff-puff as the boat slowed down to reduce noise. We were approaching the tip of the western peninsula of Halkidiki called Kassandra. It was close to 4:00 AM, and we could see light on shore, and within those lights, I spotted a light going on and off. That signal was meant for us to go toward that direction, and the captain approached slowly and carefully, looking to see if there were any German patrol boats. But the area looked safe to the captain, and we docked. A man ran out from the nearby house and came to help us. He was our contact man and was a member of the organization in Greece. We jumped out from the boat, and the man came and shook hands with us. Yiapitzoglou said to him, "This is my radio operator, an American, Helias Nikolaou." In the meantime, the captain told us not to waste too much time shaking hands. He wanted to unload the rice and other stuff from the boat and leave before daybreak. We thanked the captain and the two sailors and went inside the house our contact man was using and gave us some coffee. We asked him how would we go to Salonica, and the contact man said that there were three ways, either by horse, car or by boat. "No cars go to Salonica anymore since the partisans stopped a taxi a couple weeks ago, and took all the men and forced them to join their forces.

"Using a horse is very dangerous going through mountains passing through areas where partisans concentrate. By boat is the safest, if you find a boat, since you need a big boat for that long trip, and all the big boats are taken by the Germans." Then the contact man stopped for a while and then he said, "You are lucky today. Today a boat is leaving, which came in on Sunday, loaded with barrels of retsina (resinated wine) and bound for Salonica! The resin comes from the trees, and the people collect it and sell it to the Germans. Most of the time there are three Germans and three Greek sailors in that boat, so go and ask them to take you. The Germans, knowing how difficult it is to travel through the mountains, sometimes take civilians on the boat."

When Yiapitzoglou heard that he would have to go by German boat he immediately refused, saying that with the gold sovereigns and guns on him, he would rather go by horse or walk. Of course, he was not carrying the oilcan with the radio in it; Spyros and I were carrying it!

When I heard that there was a possibility of going by boat, I told Spyros, "Let us go, Spyros, by boat." Without thinking, Spyros got his can and followed me out the door. We thanked the contact man, and as I shook hands with Yiapitzoglou, while he told me to be careful and that if we arrived safely, he would meet us in a cafe where the boat would leave us at the end of the peninsula, and to wait for him there till he came. Then he said, "Fellows, if you succeed in bringing yourselves and the two radios to your destination using a German boat, then it will be written in history that two OSS spies transported two wireless radios while on a German cruise."

We all smiled, and as Spyros and I were walking toward the harbor to find the German boat, Spyros, who realized now what we were planning to do, turned to me and said, "Helias, do you really plan to use the German boat? Wouldn't that be very dangerous?"

I turned and said to him, "Do you have another solution? Would you rather be taken as a prisoner by the partisans? Follow me." I told him.

When we reached the harbor, we had no difficulty spotting the German patrol boat. Three Greek sailors were rolling small barrels of retsina they had bought from the locals, toward the boat.

Outside the boat were three Germans. One was a sergeant who was counting the barrels brought to the boat. When we approached, I told Spyros to wait, and then I went to the sergeant. Since I knew German I told him that for two weeks I was collecting the oil to put in the container. And since I was afraid the partisans would take it, I asked if he was kind enough to take me and my friend wherever they were going. He was also young, in his mid-twenties, and he looked at me, feeling sorry that I was runing around for two weeks, just for a can of olive oil, and said, "OK, bring your oil can inside the boat." I asked him also to take my friend, and he turned and saw Spyros who was much older, around forty-five years old. He almost said no, but then he changed his mind and said, "OK, tell him also to come." I called Spyros, who was obviously trembling inside, and he followed me inside the boat. We found an empty spot and placed the two cans adjacent to the German flag. Since nobody was around us, I asked Spyros if he realized the irony of our predicament in which two American OSS agents with three hundred gold pieces and two guns on them can transport two wireless radios using a German boat. "Stop, stop," Spyro said. "I still don't know if we did the right thing. Who knows what is going to happen when the Germans come on the boat."

"Relax," I said to Spyros. "Nothing is going to happen. Stop showing them your fear!"

"OK, Helias," Spyros said. "Maybe I was not fit to be doing these things or maybe I am too old," he said. In the meantime, the boat was ready to leave, and as I looked outside, I spotted Yiapitzoglou waving at us. He wanted to be sure we got on board before he started what would be his long tiresome trip through the mountains.

The boat left the dock, and since the sea was calm, was going very fast, keeping very close to the shore. One of the Germans approached us, and as we were passing a small village, he came and asked what was the name of that village.

I, who understood what he was asking, realized that since we were supposed to be familiar with that area and therefore should know the name of the village, immediately picked a name from the air and told the German. The name I told the German had a funny meaning—dirty town, "Vromohori". The German said, "Ya! Ya!" And as he moved away, Spyros was laughing inside and told me to avoid talking to the Germans because they might be trying to find out if we really knew the area.

As the boat was going northwards, around noon time, both Greeks and Germans began to prepare themselves for lunch. The German sergeant brought cans of food and distributed them. Our contact man, the one who had sent us to the boat, also gave us a loaf of bread and some cheese and we thought that we should also eat at the same time.

While we were cutting the bread we noticed that one of the Greek sailors was calling the German sergeant to show him our oilcans. "What is happening?" I said to Spyros, "why is the Greek sailor pointing out our cans to the sergeant?" Spyros, of course, started trembling again and immediately thought of the worst. Obviously, he said they found out that we have hidden something, in each can. "I told you Helias", Spyros said, "they would suspect that something is hidden in those cans".

"Stop" I said to Spyros "our radios in those cans are not visible. Stay calm, I am going to find out what the Greek sailor is telling the German." When I got close to them I observed that the Greek sailor was holding a big plate of sliced tomatoes and was asking the German sergeant if he could have some olive oil from the cans for their salad in exchange for the free ride we were getting. Since I had been standing next to him, the German sergeant looked at me waiting for my answer, and as soon as I realized that they only wanted some olive oil, I uncovered the spout from one of the cans and poured enough oil for his salad. The Greek thanked me and I placed the can back where it was before, next to the German flag. When I returned, Spyros was scared, sitting and trembling. "Relax" I said to Spyros "they only wanted some olive oil for their tomato salad. Calm down, nobody suspects anything, including the Germans. If the sergeant looks at you and notices that you are scared, that would be worse."

In the early afternoon, the boat was entering a harbor called Portes. We were about to get off the boat, and the Greek sailor who asked for the olive oil, volunteered to help me with the oilcan. I told him that I did not need any help, and I told him "it is only olive oil and therefore it is not that heavy". If he had lifted the cans, he might have realized it contained much more that just olive oil, and if he had made any comments about the weight of the cans, that comment would arouse suspicion to the Germans.

Early in the afternoon, we arrived at the end of the peninsula and entered the harbor of a town called Portes. We thanked the Germans, especially the sergeant who was so kind to have given us a free ride, to two desperate-looking peasants who had traveled so much for two cans of olive oil.

As we walked out, we saw a few cafes, and I reminded Spyros that Yiapitzoglou was to meet us at one of those cafes the following morning. We were very hungry, and we went to a restaurant to eat. After finishing the meal, we were told at the cashier to pay seven, which to us was not clear; did he mean seven, seven hundred, or seven thousand? We were told in training not to ask questions of familiar things. The next customer in line paying his bill gave hundreds, so we assumed our bill was seven hundred drachmas. We got it right.

Spyros said that we should find a hotel, to sleep that night. We asked at the restaurant, and they told us that there was a small hotel, except they said that in order to sleep in a hotel, we would have to give our identification cards to the German police office. Avoiding such a move, we took the cans and continued walking by the harbor looking at the boats, not knowing where to sleep during the night. We passed by a big, open tugboat where its captain was painting the end of it. Part of the boat's end was covered, and we saw a little mattress rolled at the corner. Immediately, I told Spyros, "How would you like to sleep overnight right there? Watch the cans and I will be right back." I jumped inside the boat and told the man that we were traveling to get some olive oil and that we didn't have money to pay for lodging, and would he mind if we slept overnight someplace in the covered area of the boat? The man saw the oilcans and said, "OK, you can sleep next to me, but I have the mattress for myself only. If you don't mind sleeping on top of bare wood, you can come and sleep."

"We don't mind," I said. I thanked him, and I went to inform Spyros of the comfortable night's sleep he would be expecting. We waited outside till about 9:00 PM when we saw the man preparing his mattress, then I told Spyros to get ready for a relaxing night to remember! By the time we brought our valuable cans inside the boat and put them in a corner, the tired owner was lying down; and in a few minutes, he started snoring. I turned to Spyros and said, "Choose your bed." And I showed him quite a large area of dusty bare wood floor. Spyros did not say anything and stretched himself on the floor, but with the nylon belt around him, the 150 gold pieces were piercing his back as he was lying on the wooden floor, so as he tried to find a comfortable spot, the gold pieces kept hitting the wooden floor with a thud. I told him to stop otherwise the tugboat captain might catch on that we're smuggling gold coins, and kill us for it. "Thanks for telling me," Spyros said. "If I move and turn a lot, wake me up and I will do the same for you!"

At daybreak we were awakened by much clamor and people running, and to our surprise, we saw soldiers with guns encircling all the boats. They were Bulgarian soldiers, pointing their guns at every boat. We got scared, thinking that they might be looking for us; and we asked the man who was sleeping next to us what was happening. He got up, and he asked the next boat captain, and he said that a Greek had stolen a large quantity of gasoline during the night, and the soldiers were trying to find who stole it. We also found out that the area we were in was given to Bulgarians to guard, Bulgaria being an ally of the Axis powers at that time.

A Bulgarian search group was seen to jump from boat to boat, searching for the gasoline. Immediately I thought of our two cans, and I was afraid if the Bulgarians examined the cans, and they needed olive oil, they might take it, and our wireless radios so I thought of some way to prevent them from getting in the boat. I saw some paint and the brush the man was using to paint the boat, and while the captain was talking to the next boat's captain, I poured some paint at the point where the search group would have to step to come into the boat. While I was spreading the paint, the search team came and saw the paint they had to step on. Since the entire boat was open and I was telling them we had no big gasoline containers in the boat, they left and went to the next boat. In the meantime, the captain of the boat we were in saw the spilled paint and started cursing at us that we spilled his paint and that it was so expensive. I told them that I knew how to paint and that I would help him in painting his tugboat, but he was so furious that he told us to get out and that we had caused a lot of damage to him already. I wanted to give money to him, but how could we, when last night we pretended we had no money to pay the hotel! Spyros laughed and said that our training had taught us many smart tricks to use.

We took our cans and walked toward the cafes and sat in one that was centrally located next to the boats. "We should have breakfast there and wait for Yiapitzoglou to arrive," I said. The oilcans, having only a wirelike handle, had made calluses on our hands, but as we were told, we tried not to show that they were so heavy.

As we were eating, we noticed that a German police boat had come and docked right in front of us. Three German policemen, wearing the metal police insignia on their chests, jumped out and ran toward the hotel. For a moment, we thought they were coming for us, but fortunately, the call was not for us. That scared us plenty, though, and we almost got up to leave, but where would we go? We had to wait there for Yiapitzoglou to come and find us so that the three of us could continue the trip toward Salonica, which was at least fifteen more miles away.

We ordered one coffee after another, anxiously looking for him. Sometime before noon, we spotted Yiapitzoglou, walking towards us with someone, looking around for us, too. We waved them to come to our table, and they both sat down quickly and were in an exhausted and pitiful condition. They said that they were not able to find either a car or a horse, and they were running most of the time, trying to avoid the partisans in the mountains, and the Germans on the open roads. Yiapitzoglou said that it was stupid of him not to come with us. Also, he congratulated us, and said that we would never have been able to carry the two cans and run through the mountains they had traveled. We were lucky again.

Chapter 9

- American spy, utilizing a horse-drawn cart for transportation, unexpectedly stopped and searched at a German check-point outside Salonica
- American spy, luckily avoiding suspicion and hand search inspection because he happened to look like the German guard's son
- Arrival in Salonica

Sitting in the restaurant in the town of Portes, we felt happy we had made the difficult part of the trip and hoped the remaining would not be that bad. We had a good lunch, and as we were eating, we were asking people how to go to Salonica. A man who heard us said that he had a horse drawn two-wheeled cart and he could take us up to a certain point, and there we could find a taxi to take us to Salonica. We agreed, and at that time, the guide who came with Yiapitzoglou said that he wanted to go back and try to get some rice for his family before the rice disappeared. We three—me, Yiapitzoglou, and Spyros—put the two cans of oil on the horse drawn vehicle and left.

After we had left, the driver of this horse wagon turned to us and said that he forgot to tell us that up ahead, there was a German checkpoint, an inspection post, since it was also the entrance to the airport. He said that the Germans were searching everyone thoroughly. "Sometimes they take their clothes off. I hope you don't have any contraband, do you?"

"Of course not," I said. "We only have two cans of olive oil." And as we turned to each other, and read each other's thoughts we said to ourselves, "And not to mention between us, 450 gold sovereigns, three guns and two radios in the cans!" After giving it some thought, I turned to Yiapitzoglou, and whispered "at least we should throw out the guns since we might hide the belts and the gold pieces, but the guns protrude too much and might be found." Yiapitzoglou thought a few seconds about throwing the guns out, but then he told me that the driver might be exaggerating. "Let us wait, and when we get near the German guards, let's observe the search of other people; and if we see the search is as strict as the driver says, we will give the guns to the driver."

Unfortunately, though, Yiapitzoglou had not even finished telling us his plan, when we entered an open courtyard. The German guards at the end of it were watching us coming since there was nobody else getting examined.

"It is too late to do anything anymore," I said to the others as we were caught unexpectedly.

The driver continued driving and brought his horse drawn vehicle right in front of the guards. In front of the guardhouse, there were two German guards holding guns, and inside the guardhouse must have been more guards. The driver mentioned that after the inspection, behind the guardhouse, we could find cars to drive us to Salonica.

The horse cart stopped in front of the guards, and the driver took the two cans of oil and placed them in front of the guards. One of the guards was older, around forty-five to fifty years old, and the other guard was young, not more that twenty to twenty-two years old.

The older guard came close, and I told him the cans contained olive oil, and he unscrewed the top and put his finger in to verify that. Since I was next to him, he told me to take my jacket off, which I did; and then he came to search me.

At that point, I thought my heartbeat had doubled, but I tried to remain calm. Let us not forget that there was nothing more than my shirt that was covering my nylon belt with the 150 gold pieces and a .32 caliber gun at the right pocket. As the German came to put his hands under my arms on each side of me and I lifted my arms a little, he stopped and stared at me attentively for a few seconds as if he recognized me, or something on me, which gave me chills, and I asked myself why was he staring at me. To my surprise, he stopped moving his hands; and as he was looking at me, he asked me, "How old are you?" I said twenty. He took his hand from me and said that he had a son eighteen years old who had been taken in the German army six months ago, and he assumed that he was sent to the Russian front. He said that I looked just like his son—the same hair, the same eyes, the same height. And then, as he went to finish his search, he put his hand on my two sides, and looking at my hair and the top of my head as if he thought he was looking and touching his son, he let his hands go down; and that's when his left hand hit the gun which was on my right side. But having his son on his mind, he probably thought he hit my belt, and then he took his hands away, still looking at my hair.

At that point, he was so moved thinking he was touching his son that I noticed a tear coming from his eye, which was also noticed by the other German, who felt like crying, too. At that point, I got encouraged. I touched the German on the shoulder and told him that the war would end soon and that his son would come home safe. He said, "Let us hope so." And trying to finish the search, he moved to Spyros, who was standing like a statue, obviously trembling from fear. He searched him a little at the sides but not around the belt and took his hands away. Then he turned to me and asked me if Yiapitzoglou was with me, and I said yes. "Go ahead," he said. And taking our cans, we moved away, robot-like, saying nothing. At about one hundred feet away, Yiapitzoglou turned to us and said, "Fellows, it was a miracle. Yes, it was a miracle that Helias looked like his son, that saved us!"

"Yes, it was a miracle," Spyros also said. "But what would have happened if the guard had started at me first?" Spyros said.

Then Spyros started moving strangely, opening his legs sideways, and finally he said, "Fellows, you have to excuse me. I need to change. I have wet my underwear!" We laughed about Spyros but we tried not to make fun of him; after all, it was an extremely scary episode, and we were very lucky again that we were not caught.

"By the way, Helias," Yiapitzoglou said, "where did you learn the German language so well?" I told them that as a high school student in Crete, I was excused from one week of forced labor per month, "If I was taking German lessons, so I had agreed to learn German, and I had attended about six months of German lessons, which helped me to speak a little," I said. "As far as we are concerned," Yiapitzoglou said, "you did extremely well. As a matter of fact, we are alive and free right now because of your German and also because you look like the German guard's son. Maybe God wanted it that way; it is a sign from Him that we will succeed on our mission."

After we passed the restricted area around the airport, we found stores, restaurants, and car stations. We saw a taxi coming toward us, and Yiapitzoglou went to hire it when he was told that two merchants had engaged it previously. And Yiapitzoglou became very sad that he had lost the taxi. "Do you want me to get that taxi?" I said. "Just watch." I went to the driver and said to him, "How much did the merchants pay you?"

He said, "Five thousand drachmas."

"Suppose I give you ten thousand drachmas, would you take us?"

"Yes," he said, "tell your friends by the time I've filled up with gas to jump in the car. I will take you instead. After all, the merchants did not pay me yet."

At the proper time, we jumped in the car and left while the merchants were chasing and cursing us. During the trip to Salonica, we asked the driver if there would be another checkpoint, and he said there was one, but only for collecting fees for imported products. "For the two oilcans, you may have to pay about one thousand drachmas."

"How would you avoid going through the checkpoint?" I asked. "Is there another way?"

"There is another way, but I did it another time, and it almost broke my car," the driver said.

"Well," I said, "suppose I give you another two thousand drachmas, would you bypass the checkpoint?" When he heard that he would make another two thousand drachmas, he agreed; and when the proper time came, he went through rough roads, which gave us a very uncomfortable ride. As we were getting away from the checkpoint, the checkpoint inspectors spotted us. They caught us and stopped us and started hitting the driver. "Stop, stop," I told them. "What is the trouble? How much would you like to stop this fight?" They looked and saw only two cans of oil, so they said, "One thousand drachmas."

"Does it pay to fight for one thousand drachmas?" I said. "Take two thousand drachmas and let us continue our trip." They took the two thousand drachmas, and they warned the taxi driver that next time he did that again they would destroy his car.

"Didn't I tell you?" the driver told us, and he was sorry he had listened to us to try to avoid the checkpoint. "Don't worry," I said to him. "Because of the aggravation you had, instead of two thousand drachmas we will give you three thousand drachmas." This made the driver feel better.

At that point, Yiapitzoglou turned to me and whispered to me, smiling, that I knew how to resolve things with the organization's money. "Why not," I said? "That is why they gave me the money."

Within a few minutes, we entered Salonica; and Yiapitzoglou told me that at a certain point near the famous Aspro Kastro, or White Castle, there was a pastry shop. I should come out from the car and wait in that pastry shop until he came back to pick me up. I should not leave no matter how long he would take to come and pick me up. He would take the oilcan with him. As I was admiring the handsomely decorated stores, I spotted the White Castle; and the car stopped in front of a centrally located pastry shop. I realized that this was the place where I had to wait and so I got out, and the car left. Immediately I realized I had not said good-bye to Spyros or to wish him good luck on his mission. For over a month we were together and had skirted many dangerous times; and in our haste, we did not even say good-bye. I never heard from him again.

Chapter 10

- The American spy finally arrives in Salonica, and after three hours of waiting in a pastry shop, is finally picked up
- Rental of a partially bombed-out, empty textile factory which becomes the "front" for the wireless cell
- Close call with German officers living next door, who sat down to play bridge while the author was installing the wireless' antenna in the factory

Cosmas Yiapitzoglou

The American Spy, Corporal Helias Doundoulakis, with civilian clothes, during mission in Salonica Greece

Getting out from the car I entered the pastry shop and since it had tables on the sidewalk I went and occupied an empty table in the front. Immediately a waiter came, stood in front of me and, as a soldier in the attention position, he said, "Yes, Sir, can I have your order please!"

"A slice of Greek cake, please," I said.

While I was eating the cake I realized that in front of me were passing more Germans than civilians. The OSS decision that they had changed their mind to drop me by parachute, outside from the city, due to the fact that there were too many Germans in Salonica area, was well justified.

I hardly had finished that slice of Greek cake when the same waiter came and asked me again if I would like another slice. I realized that since I was occupying the best sidewalk table, the waiter demanded that either I continue ordering another sweet, or leave, or at least sit at an interior table. It was interesting, or rather funny, that since I was forced to wait for over three and a half hours, I had eaten over six slices of cake until my stomach started hurting, and I felt sick and ready to throw up.

Just them, suddenly I heard someone at the next table say, "Helias, come here." I turned my head toward the voice and saw a stranger with black sunglasses calling me.

I went to his table, and he introduced himself as Nicos Oreopoulos. He apologized for being so late to come and get me, but he had to find me a place to stay before he came. "I hope you tried the pastas here. They claim they are the best in town," Nicos said.

"Oh, yes," I said. "They were so delicious that I was forced to eat six of them."

Nicos, without analyzing my answer, replied, "They were really that good?"

Nicos told me to get up and go; and as we were moving away from the table, I noticed that the waiter was bringing me another pasta, and at this time, I turned to him and told him to sit down and eat it himself because I'd had enough pastas for one day, which he eagerly obliged, and agreed that they were the best in town.

As Nicos and I walked out, I turned to him and voiced my concern that there were more . . . Germans than civilians. He told me not to be afraid of the German soldiers. What I should fear, however, is the German police, the SS (Schutzstaffel), and the Greek secret police.

"I was told," Nicos said, "that you are an American soldier, most likely the only American soldier in Salonica, and the German police would really be happy to get their hands on you."

Nicos said he had found me a temporary place to stay till he found me a better more permanent place. The temporary quarters were at the top of the city, a house with a magnificent view, but as I found out in that area, there were many communists; and every time the Germans wanted hostages, they used that area to get the hostages, So Nicos said that I should not stay there too long.

Nicos had asked me what type of a building he should find to install the wireless, and I told him that it should be at least fifty feet long since the length of the antenna pointing southward should be at least fifty feet. So he went looking for buildings that long.

During the following days, Nicos told me he had found a deserted textile factory, once owned by Greek Jews, semi-destroyed and not utilized by anyone, and since it was very long, it would be perfect for our purposes. We visited the place. The main factory was a very large room without partitions and had big windows on each side. At the end, there were two rooms with windows and doors. It had a very big courtyard, at least seventy-five feet long and the main entrance was as large, with a tremendous steel gate. At the corner, there was also a two-room apartment where an old lady lived. After we examined the place, I told Nicos it would be ideal for my job. I also suggested to buy wood, coal, oil, and petroleum and pretend we had business to sell that stuff.

"Perfect idea," Nicos said. "I will ask around the town if they could rent the place for us and then tell Yiapitzoglou to give us money to buy the stuff."

As we left the place, Nicos said to me, "I forgot to tell you. I have found a place for you to stay permanently. Why don't I take you there right now and show you the place? As a matter of fact, it is very close to here, and if we get this factory for the wireless, it would be very convenient for you." We walked not far from the factory, and we entered a courtyard where there were three separate apartments. One of them had three rooms and was occupied by a lady with three little kids and her mother. The husband of the lady, as I was told, was a Greek officer and was killed in Albania during the Greco-Italian campaign. The three apartments belonged to Greek Jews before, and since they were forced to flee, the authorities had given these apartments to refugees. As we entered the house, Nicos introduced me to the lady, and then they showed me the room in which I would be staying. It was obvious that they had painstakingly made their living room my bedroom! Since that family had no income during the German occupation, I was told by Nicos that instead of paying rent to them I could just give them money daily for their food, and I could eat with them.

The mother of the kids, who had become a widow at the age of twenty-eight, was very attractive and obviously a close companion to Nicos up to that day. As we were leaving, Nicos turned to me and said, "Helias, you are a lucky guy. What other sacrifices shall I do for Greece?" At the beginning, I did not understand what he meant; but later on, I found out. Under Yiapitzoglou's orders, Nicos was surrendering the girl of his desires to me, for the safety of the organization, in order that I would not have to chase girls outside and expose myself to danger. Yiapitzoglou felt that a girlfriend in the house would be a lot safer, so the pretty young widow of only twenty-eight years old, who was nicknamed "Sultanitsa" would provide subsistence for a family of five while she would offer her charms and friendship to me. A very desirable deal, I thought, so the arrangement was that I would leave money on the table every day for the family to buy food; and I would have breakfast and supper every day with them, except lunch. In the meantime, I would be welcomed with the charms of the attractive Sultanitsa, who was dressing up quite attractively every afternoon to welcome me.

Nicos had inquired about the factory, and the city was willing to rent it to us. We, three of us—Yiapitzoglou, Nicos, and I—met at a cafe and mentioned to Yiapitzoglou our plan to convert the place into a wholesale-business store, where we would be selling coal, oil, firewood, and other products; and he liked the idea very much, a place that would not rouse much suspicion. We would spend around $10,000 for the above mentioned things and pretend to sell only wholesale. I suggested that we should sell at higher prices than others, in order to minimize incoming customers. At that suggestion of mine, Nicos, who was a merchant in real life, interrupted me, saying, "The war is teaching us new rules to do business, a system never heard of—to sell at higher prices to chase the customers away!" We all laughed at his comment, but would suit our purposes just fine.

The following day, we paid some money to the city, and we got a key for the place. Nicos and I examined the factory, which, as we were told, was a Jewish textile factory and provided work for many people before the war. When the Germans came, they destroyed it. The factory itself was over seventy-five feet in length by twenty-five feet wide. It had very big glass windows, but now they were all down and open.

In the front of the factory, and near the gate entrance, were two rooms or offices with large windows and glass doors. A large courtyard connected the factory entrance to the main street, blocked by an oversized iron gate. When I examined the place, my first impression was that it was excellent. We had a place which could accommodate the exact specifications for the antenna, and an ideal location to install the wireless with and excellent vantage point. I told Nicos to buy me over one hundred feet of antenna wire. That afternoon, we three met again; and we told Yiapitzoglou that we had visited the factory and that we had found it to be ideal.

Yiapitzoglou told us that we would have two guards who would be in the factory at all times, pretending to be salesmen. He said he had ordered a full truckload of firewood, which he would dump inside the front iron gate at the courtyard. At the time, I would be operating the wireless, Yiapitzoglou said, one of the watchmen would be just inside the front gate, pretending he would be cutting the wood; but his job would be to watch toward the street, watching who was walking by and who was coming toward the gate and inform Helias about any intruders. The second watchman, at the time I would be operating the wireless, would be walking around the block of the factory and be alert to whatever strange trucks or cars were observed. He said that two watchmen should be sufficient, but the number could be increased in the future if needed.

In the meantime, Nicos told me he had bought me 150 feet of antenna wire; and I was planning to go the following day to install the antenna if they sent one of the watchmen to help me do that.

The next day, having the wire with me, I tried to figure out how to install it so that it was concealed.

The factory had an A frame metal roof and horizontal beams fifteen feet above its concrete floor. Each framework was about 3.5 feet away from the next one, so that, *if we could climb to the first horizontal beam then by jumping from beam to beam and pulling the antenna wire, we could install the needed antenna with no problem.* At 10:00 AM, I was in the factory and until 2:00 PM I was waiting in vain for the watchman to come and help me, but he never showed. So I decided to go up and install the antenna by myself. I found some boxes, and by putting them one on top of the other, I climbed on the first horizontal beam of the factory framework. I felt that I could hide the wire on the wall at the end of the horizontal beams. In the meantime, I was pulling the end of the antenna wire. I jumped to the second beam and said to myself that I should try to finish this installation fast since I could be spotted easily and . . . they would no doubt suspect immediately what I was trying to do.

While I was standing on the second beam and trying to hide the wire by the wall, I heard people talking, and next to me there was a very large window, all broken, and I saw four German officers of various ranks. They were carrying a bridge table and four chairs, which they placed right under me; and then they sat down to play bridge since it was a nice shady area. I knew that every big house, which had two extra rooms and an additional bathroom had to accommodate the German authorities, particularly the officers. The house next to the factory had those provisions, and those German officers were living in that house. Knowing that the building was empty, they would suspect foul play immediately. All they had to do was look up.

In order to hide, I moved behind a column, and I was standing mostly on one leg. I said to myself, *How long would I be able to stand like this up here without them noticing me?* Since it was so dusty up there, what would happen if I sneezed or coughed? I was so close to them, right above them in fact that, since I knew how to play bridge, I was following their game and judging their plays and mistakes.

My God, I said to myself. *Is this the way I should terminate my mission, getting caught before I had the chance to send even a single message? What would Major Vassos say? I survived the German inspection, which was miraculous, and now that I am ready to begin my mission, I will be caught like a mouse in a trap, because four German officers decided to play bridge.* Then I thought to myself that I will not get caught, I will not cough or sneeze, and I will not move from this standing on-one-leg position no matter how many hours it would take!

As I was pushing my head on the wall trying to hide behind the vertical column, I realized that I had put my head inside a spider web, and a large spider (more than one inch long) was an inch or two away from my face. I blew the spider away which seemed to be angry from the destruction of its web, and I was afraid I would be bitten by the spider any moment, so I moved my right hand slowly, and tore and threw the spider web away from my face. By doing that the wind took the web towards the broken open window area that was next to me, and blew it on the top of the bridge table on which the German officers were playing bridge! One German picked up the web, looked upwards to see where it came from and with some German curse he threw it away from the table. Fortunately he did not see me and nothing serious happened except the destruction of a very well made spider web.

From 2:00 PM, time was moving very slowly till at about 5:00 PM; a siren was heard, for supper at 5:30 PM. Though they had heard the siren, they continued the game till they had finished the hand at the game, and when they got up, they took the table and chairs and went inside the house. I thanked God that again I was able to survive the situation, and I started moving my legs, which seemed to feel paralyzed. I kicked my legs a few times, and with difficulty, I tried to walk after having been in that standing-on-one-leg position for close to three and a half hours.

I said to myself that I was not able to continue, so I wanted to go back to the first beam and climb down using the boxes I had piled up under the first beam. As I tried to jump from the second beam to the first, I realized I had no power in my legs to do that so I fell, but by falling, I hit my head on the first beam. And as I turned, I fell facedown, fifteen feet to the concrete floor below. I must have lost consciousness as I hit my face on the floor, and when I awoke, I saw much blood on the floor. I had broken my nose as my face hit the ground.

With nose broken and bloodied, I went to my landlady who let out a high-pitched scream when she saw me. She wanted me to go to the hospital, which of course I refused to do. I told her that a piece of wood fell and hit my nose and if she brought me some ice and gave me just a kiss, I would be OK. In a short time, truthfully enough, she not only gave me ice but other remedies that in a short time, I felt wonderful. I had forgotten that scary experience, and for that tender and quickly curing treatment of Sultanitsa, I wouldn't have minded repeating another fall!

I met Yiapitzoglou that night and told him what had happened, and he could not believe what he was hearing. We had achieved our goal of coming to Salonica, experiencing so many dangerous situations only to be caught because four Germans wanted to play bridge. Also, he could not believe that I was able to remain motionless for three and a half hours without a cough or sneeze. He was cursing the watchman who was supposed to come and help me for the installation of the antenna wire. "Tomorrow I will send both of them, and you should only tell them what to do; you should not go up there again. I have to watch you more," Yiapitzoglou said. "For your interest, besides for the interest of the organization. What would I do without such a lucky guy like you who has miraculously avoided capture so many times in the past three weeks. Either you had been trained extremely well to avoid capture, or God is on your side, and of course, on ours," Yiapitzoglou said. And he squeezed my arm. Having installed the antenna, I told Nicos that we should find a place to hide the wireless, the battery, and whatever other articles we would use. Also, I had in mind to have on the table, next to the wireless a .45 caliber gun, my gun I had brought from Cairo, and a couple of grenades to be used in case the Germans raided the place at the time I would be sending my messages. The factory was empty and you could only see a pile of lint or pieces of materials at one corner, nothing else. In the two rooms, there was one table, which we would use to put the radio and the guns on, but no closets or other furniture were in any other place. We had to find a better place to hide the radio, so as I was going inside the factory and as I walked past the lint with my shoes, I kicked a plywood board quite by accident under the pile of lint. I tried to lift the plywood with my hands and saw there was a large hole in the floor. I called Nicos and we both lifted the plywood, and to our surprise, we found a wonderful hiding place. Explaining that to Yiapitzoglou, he came up with a possible purpose of that hole, that since the owners of the factory were Jewish and were forced to leave, they probably had hidden a large quantity of gold sovereigns there, knowing that they would not be able to take the gold with them. Greeks, or possibly Germans, suspecting that gold must be hidden there, searched and found the hiding place and later took everything.

We determined to use that hole for hiding the radio and everything else, since if we kept that pile of lint covering the plywood, nobody would know what was under there, unless of course, someone knew about that hole and came back to see if we had hidden anything there, now that we used the factory for our business. Since we had no other hiding place, we decided to use it though there were no doors to prevent anybody from coming in the factory area anytime while we were not there. The following day, Nicos brought the wireless and the battery; and I set up the table with what I should need before starting to make contact with Cairo. I had brought the antenna down from the roof, and its end was hidden and could be pulled out only during the wireless operation. I placed the table in such a position in the small room that I could look outside the courtyard and see the watchman who would watch the gate. Though I could see outside, anyone in the courtyard looking through the glass door, could see me with the radio. To prevent that, I thought of hanging curtains on the glass door, which I did not want either, since the curtains would prevent me from seeing outwards. Also, if someone rushed in through the gate and the watchman could not stop him, he would immediately see me with the headphones on. How would I be able to escape? I only had a low glass window in the adjacent small room, facing a big yard where the German officers were staying. So I had decided that the only way to escape if, let us say, the Germans raided us, was to jump through the small window into the next door neighbor's yard and try to run outside using their fence door, which was on another street. For that, I had cut the window frame all around with a knife so that the glass was barely standing in its place and would easily fall out if a small push was exerted on it by me. I was more comfortable with that escape plan. I might delay rushing Germans also by throwing a couple of grenades prior to my escape.

The day we were supposed to have the first contact, the two watchmen were present, and the table was set with the wireless on top of it. We had agreed in Cairo that every day at 3:00 PM, they would give me a signal in order to make the first contact. It was only 1:00 PM, and all of us were nervous for our first communication with OSS in Cairo. I saw Yiapitzoglou talking to Nicos Oreopoulos in an uneasy way and the watchman Stavros to be at his post, which was to be inside the iron gate, pretending to cut firewood; but his job would be to scour the passersby. Nikitas, the other watchman would be walking around the block, alert to what would be happening, and if he spotted German trucks or cars coming to run fast and inform me to stop transmission and try to escape.

We had not sent any messages yet since I was told that the city of Salonica was more important than Athens for the concentration and movement of German troops in it, and for that, it should be watched extremely well by the German Gestapo. *What would happen as soon as I go on the air? Would the German triangulation instruments find me immediately and would they come to get me?*

All these thoughts raced through our minds, and that was why we all were very nervous. In the meantime, I had put the table in the proper place, and we placed the wireless on it, and the battery under the table. And then I placed the two guns, one .45 caliber and next to it the .32 caliber, which I had brought from Cairo and next to them a small wooden box with two grenades in it. All that time, Yiapitzoglou and Nicos Oreopoulos were watching me; and I saw their expressions looking a little scared in case someone happened to come in and see all that on the table. He would not need other proof to guess what we were supposed to be doing.

I walked outside the yard and told Nikitas that fifteen minutes before transmitting, he would go outside and check the block and continue circling the block till Stavros, the watchman inside the gate, informed him that the transmission had ended. I also saw Mrs. Eleni, the woman who was living in the two-room gated apartment and asked her if she wanted oil, petroleum, or firewood; and she said no. After all, she said, "I have not seen any customers buying anything in here yet." We told her not to worry since we were selling wholesale, and that was why she had not seen any customers coming to buy things. Of course, she did not know she was sitting on the top of a pile of dynamite. If the Germans raided our place with guns and I was throwing hand grenades, Mrs. Eleni would be in the middle of everything. I felt sorry for not being able to warn her, but on the other hand, we were hoping nothing would happen. It was five minutes to 3:00 PM, and everyone saw me putting my headphones on and listening for the signal.

At exactly 3:00 PM, I heard someone calling, "Cando, Cando," which was my name. I told them, "Hear it." They said, "Cando." "What is Cando?" they said. I put the headphones on everyone's ear, and they all heard, -.-, .-, -., -.., ---, which in Morse code is "Cando."

I told them that in Cairo they had asked me what name would they call to identify me, so while I was hesitating to find some name, the sergeant asked me what city was I born in America; and I said Canton, Ohio, so the sergeant said, "In the air we will call you Canto, or better yet, Cando."

It is strange, I said to them, but what you hear in the air now is my name. Even the Germans hear it right now and they are saying to themselves: Who is Cando?

"My god, Oreopoulos said, we learn a lot of things in this war! To me it is only a noise in the air, to you it means we have made contact with Cairo."

The picture shows the wireless on table and author at center, at the left side Nicos Oreopoulos. and Cosmas Yiapitzoglou, at the right side, the 2 guards, Stavros and Nikitas

Chapter 11

- Communication established with Cairo and messages sent daily
- Access to valuable information and sent messages resulted in the sinking many ships, killing thousands of Germans
- Receipt of information of departure of three thousand Germans, and transmission of information to OSS resulted in twelve American airplanes bombing the railroad station and killing 2,500 Germans

"As you can see, fellas, we have made contact with Cairo, we have established communication."

"We are in business," I said, and everyone smiled.

I replied to Cairo and set up 10:00 AM the following day as the next contact. In the meantime, Yiapitzoglou had a small introductory message to send, which I sent with no difficulty.

We all were happy, we saw that nothing had gone wrong, and we all felt confident nothing would happen to jeopardize the operation.

In the meantime, Yiapitzoglou had contacted many friends he thought would be able to collect information on German movements. And according to the location of their workplaces, he had divided them in groups. People who were working in the harbor area would be responsible for ships leaving the harbor, people working in the airport or railroad stations would inform us whatever they observed also. He had people who were cleaning the floors and toilets in various German offices who had agreed to provide us with information. In general, Yiapitzoglou had many groups of friends in many locations and organizations in the city. Each group had a representative who was collecting the information and who then notified Yiapitzoglou of the news, such as a ship getting ready to leave, a train loaded with troops or hostages that were caught, how many and where they were being kept to name a few. After Yiapitzoglou collected the information, it would be up to him to judge what was important to be sent to Cairo, and he would give it to me. I would divide the news into messages with at least twenty-five words each, code them, and send them. I was told not to send more than one, the most would be two messages at a time, if they were short. During the training period in Cairo, we were told that while we were sending "telegrams" we would be heard also by the Gestapo whose triangulation instruments could give them our position. Because of that, we were told that sending one telegram was not so dangerous, but sending two telegrams was inviting the Gestapo for dinner. Sending three telegrams, one right after the other, was digging your own grave. I had been warned that since I was given three frequencies to use at my discretion, I could change frequencies for every new telegram I was planning to send if I needed to send three messages at once.

After a while my job using the wireless had become routine, none of us were afraid anymore. As a matter of fact, everyone around the neighborhood knew we had rented the place and were running a black market business selling different merchandise, like petroleum, coal, olive oil, wood and other items. Our neighbors on the left, right and across the street would greet us every time we would go out or come in. They were especially nice to me, and they were impressed by a young man who was running a successful business by himself.

We had not only become friendly with the neighbors, but I also became friendly with German officers living next door. These German officers would play bridge two to three times a week in between their building and my building. They had realized we were using the factory for a business, and I was not afraid to approach them and talk to them as a businessman. I cut the framing from a small window that I was going to use as an escape route in case the Gestapo raided the factory to arrest me. This window was near the table the German officers were using to play bridge. One day I had finished sending two telegrams to Cairo and I had put everything securely away. I heard four German officers outside from my window who had come to play their game of bridge. I went and opened the small window and said hello to them in German. I said "I see you play bridge, I also play bridge". They replied by saying if they ever needed a 4th they would ask me to join them.

I filled up a dish with almonds and walnuts and gave it to them, which they appreciated very much with many "Dankaschoens". Our group met in a cafe bar that evening, and I told them about my conversation with the German officers and we all laughed about it.

The information I was sending to Cairo, was coming from all over Salonica, the harbor, rail road, airports and I was having two contacts with Cairo daily, one about 10:00 AM and another at three or four o'clock in the afternoon, sending one or two telegrams each time. OSS Cairo was interested a lot in ship departures, especially if the ships had troops leaving the harbor. We would tell them what the ships were getting loaded with and the time the ships would leave the harbor so that Allied ships or airplanes would find them out from Salonica harbor and sink them. Many ships went to the bottom of the Mediterranean with our assistance.

Since everything was going so easily, we had forgotten the danger we were in. We used to meet a couple of times a week in a waterfront tavern and drink to our successful continuation. One afternoon after I had sent three telegrams, Yiapitzoglou said to me and Nicos that we deserved to go and have a couple of drinks at the waterfront tavern. We had ordered plenty of appetizers, shrimp, clams, and french fried potatoes, along with Greek Ouzo. During the German occupation people were dying of hunger; nobody could find work and food was very scarce. A group of elderly people passed close to where we were sitting, and as soon as they saw the food we had on our table, they looked at us with such hostility, thinking that we must be German collaborators saying to us aloud that the "day will come soon when you the traitors will pay with your lives."

How ironic, that we were endangering ourselves daily in order that peace would come sooner, but saying anything to these people would serve no purpose.

I did not have to acquire or steal the information, as I was trained in the spy academy because the information was coming to me freely. After I had sent the telegrams in the morning or afternoon, I was able to spend the rest of the time as I pleased, so I was going three times a week to learn how to dance in a dance school or go swimming at the Alexander the Great public swimming pool where I was asked by two German officers where I got my American watch.

Another pleasant preoccupation every day was that since I had plenty of money to spend, I could find special food for the family I was staying with. I would buy it and bring it home, so all the neighbors were looking at me with awe. Besides, my landlady bragged to her neighbors about their enterprising tenant, that while this young man had his own business, their husbands had none.

Across the street, a university professor lived with his wife and their eighteen-year-old daughter named Annoula. The mother obviously persuaded her daughter to get friendly with me, so Annoula would wait all day for me to come home in the afternoon to sing Greek songs under my window to attract my attention, an action that irritated my attractive jealous landlady, Sultanitsa. At the beginning, I tried not pay attention to Annoula and her friends, not wanting to aggravate Sultanitsa, who in the meantime was trying so hard with all her majestic powers to please me, so I did not even open the window. I remembered the girl's disappointed expression for neglecting them. But since they were very persistent to serenade me and more importantly since Annoula was extremely beautiful and charming, I finally opened the window and saw their faces sparkle with pleasure that I had finally surrendered to their siren-like singing. But what could I do, should I also sing with them? Ordinarily, Romeo was singing below and Juliet was above. Would I reverse the situation in my case and start singing for them from above? *No*, I said to myself, *it would not be proper. I should have a musical instrument.* And by playing the musical instrument above, the girls would sing below. So I had to find a musical instrument.

From early on, I dreamt to play the accordion; but since it was very expensive to buy an accordion in those days, I had kept it only in my dreams.

In Salonica one day, as I was walking in a well-known market avenue named Tsimisky, I had seen an accordion in the window of a music store, so I went to that store hoping to still see it in that window. I went, and to my satisfaction, it was still there. I went inside and asked the salesman for the price. He looked at me and thought I could not possibly have much money and said that the accordion was not for sale. "Why not?" I said. "I have money." To get rid of me, he told me to speak to the manager in the office. The manager looked at me and said to me that he admired me for my choice. And he told me that when he was the same age, he wanted to play the accordion. Because of that, he got involved with other instruments, and later on, he began selling them. "This accordion you see in my window, my boy," he told me, "is the only one left in my store and in the entire city of Salonica. It is a very precious instrument, and since it is the only one for sale in our city, it costs many gold sovereigns. I know you would like to have it, but you cannot possibly have the money to buy it."

"How many gold sovereigns would you sell it for?" I asked. "I have gold sovereigns."

"Really?" he said. And with a smile in his face thinking that I would be surprised when I heard it, he said, "Twenty gold pieces for the accordion and two gold pieces for the case!" And he expected me to turn around and leave, but he was very surprised when he heard me saying, "OK, I will bring you twenty gold pieces tomorrow and get it."

While I was going out, he and the salesman were staring at me, wondering if I really was serious or simply joking.

Leaving the store, I looked at the accordion as if it were mine already.

As I walked toward the theater area, I suddenly saw Annoula, the girl who was serenading me every day, together with her parents. There was a show in one of the theaters that was advertised to give its premiere performance that night, and there were many people buying tickets for that night's performance. Annoula introduced me to her father and at the same time her mother turned to her father and said to him that I was the boy across the street, the business-minded boy she had talked about many times. I asked them if they were planning to go to the theater that evening, and the father said that they wanted to see that show; but unfortunately, he said, they were too late and all the tickets were sold. Their faces were very disappointed since they wanted very much to see that show's premiere. I asked them to wait and I would try to get them tickets. "No," the father said, "I had asked, and they are all sold out." I said again if they wanted to wait, I would get tickets, and I went to the ticket office. The price of the tickets ordinarily was five hundred drachmas. I took ten thousand drachmas and put them on the window and said, "Please give me only four tickets for all this money." The manager saw the money and immediately said to his helper, "Give four extra tickets to the gentleman and go and put four chairs in the front." When I showed the professor the four tickets, he could not believe it. I told them I happened to know the manager, and that was the reason why I got the tickets, so we all went inside to see the show. Since the four special chairs were put in the very front, everybody, including the actors were wondering who we were.

That night I told Yiapitzoglou that I needed twenty-five sovereigns and that he should bring them to me in the morning. "Twenty-five," he said. "What are you going to do with so many of them?"

"I am buying an accordion," I said. Of course, he did not expect to hear such an answer, and with a very loud voice, he said, "What?"

"You are buying an accordion, did I hear it right? he said. "The Gestapo is looking for us, and they would be willing to kill hundreds of Greek people in order to find the only American soldier in Salonica right now, and instead of hiding as much as you can, you are thinking of serenading? Obviously, you don't realize the danger you are in. Just because they have not caught you yet, it does not mean they wouldn't hear you tomorrow and come for you.

"Do you know that with twenty-five sovereigns, you could buy an apartment now when people are starving, or a house, the ones the Jewish people left behind?"

He was expecting me to say that I was just kidding or joking for saying such a stupid thing, but he had not realized that I was so obsessed with the accordion. Anyway, it would help us forget our dangerous lives, I told him.

"I know what you are saying," I told him. "But I own over one hundred gold pieces, and who knows, I may be killed tomorrow, and what would these sovereigns do for me when I am dead? I want to enjoy them now that I am still alive."

Yiapitzoglou, seeing that I had made up my mind to get the accordion and especially when he thought of my last sentence, he told me very regretfully that if that is what would make me happy, he would bring me twenty-five gold pieces the following morning with a promise that I would not expose myself to unnecessary danger by playing the accordion too excessively out in the open. Obviously, he must have agreed with me, why not enjoy my life while I was still alive!

Next day after having sent two messages to Cairo, I went to the music store and directly entered the office. Both the salesman and the manager were watching me and waited to see what I would do, and with a big surprise, they saw me putting twenty-two gold pieces on the table.

"My boy," the manager said, "I am not asking you where you found so many gold pieces, but since you brought me what I asked for, the accordion is yours."

The salesman put that beautiful brand-new Hohner accordion in its case and gave it to me. "Enjoy it," the manager said. "But please don't tell anyone how much you paid for it if they ask you." Obviously, he had overcharged me so much that he did not want anybody to hear about that sale.

I also understood that what I had paid was an exorbitant price, but for me, a peasant boy who in a short time had his pockets laced with gold and was not sure if he would be alive for long to enjoy it, it did not matter. I wanted to enjoy life at any price. So I took the accordion to the house where I was staying, and at the beginning, I could not even strap it on. Yiapitzoglou and I then adjusted the straps and I started playing by ear some familiar Greek songs. Now it was a good match, me playing the accordion on the top, on an open window and the girls singing right below.

The entire neighborhood began talking about the successful young businessman with the accordion. My landlady, of course, jealous of the other girls especially Anoula, objected to the daily singing and complained to Nicos Oreopoulos. Oreopoulos told Yiapitzoglou what was going on, and they arranged a meeting, explaining to me that some neighbors liked the singing, others didn't, so the ones who did not appreciate my singing, could complain, to perhaps the Greek Police, and who knows where that could have gone. So they made me understand that I should have no more singing concerts, and if I liked the girls outside my window, why not ask and take them out instead. So that ended the concerts. And my landlady, Sultanitsa, could not be any happier!

One day there happened to be an identification inspection by the German police, and I had to show my I.D. to them, which they accepted without question. It was the identification I had been given in Smyrna, Turkey, which indicated a certain unidentified address as my residence. Up to that date,

I had never looked to see what address they had put down. Why I never looked always bothers me even today. I was only twenty years old, trained to become a spy, and by behaving wildly in many ways, I had not acted as a sensible adult. I was having the time of my life, and as Nicos Oreopoulos said, **"For you, Helias, the war should never end, you will never have it better than now!"**

Having realized that I had not checked my fake address, I went there, and I could not believe my eyes; it was a hotel waterfront building in which many people, including German soldiers, were going in and out. *My God,* I said to myself, *I'm supposed to be living in here?* When they gave me the fake identification in Smyrna, Turkey, I had asked the sergeant, what address had they put as my residence; and he said they had picked up an address from a telephone book. He did not know himself where that house was, so he suggested that as soon as I had found a place to stay in Salonica, I should try to get a legal one. Now, having an identification showing an address that could very easily be a German police office, I became very worried. I knew that I had to get a new identification as soon as possible, but until I got a new identification, at least I should change the number of the house to represent a more common residence instead of a hotel. It should be a number representing a smaller house. Walking farther down the street, I found a better number, and when I went home with an eraser, I tried to erase the number that was on my identification to insert the new one, but instead I made a small hole on my identification. *Now,* I said to myself, *I am worse off. Anyone looking at my identification would realize there is something wrong with it. I have to get a new identification immediately!*

I called Yiapitzoglou and told him my new achievements, and he agreed that they should find a way to get me a new legal identification. He suggested that until we got a new I.D., I should try to limit my exposure and confine myself to my apartment.

Two weeks had passed and Oreopoulos was searching to find a trusted individual working in the office of issuing identifications to be willing to give a stranger a legal identification. Finally, we were informed that one of our members had a relative in that office and he was going to approach him to do this forbidden action. While I was anxiously waiting to find out if it could be done, one day while on a streetcar, I was coming to the last exit in the center of the city, and the conductor told everyone to have their identifications ready since the German police were looking for partisans again, and everyone would be checked. *What now? Suppose they see the hole in my identification?* I had no more time to think about it, and the German policeman entered the streetcar. I took my identification, covering the hole with my finger and showed it to the German who simply looked at it. He looked at me, seeing an innocent-looking young man, far different from a face of a partisan he was searching for, and moved to the next passenger. *It was a close call again.*

The following week, Oreopoulos told me that he had found an inside man, and he told me that I should go to a certain office exactly at twelve noon the following day at the number two window, and say Helias. My friend Oreopoulos had given him a picture, the name, Helias Nicolaou, and the address Serron 10, Salonica, which was my actual residence. The following day at twelve noon, I went to window number two; and there was a man wearing a big visor above his eyes, and I said, "Helias." And without raising his head to look at me, he pushed a paper toward me to sign. I saw that he had already filled up my name, address, and everything else. After I signed it, he took it, stamped it, signed it, and he came back and gave it to me.

In all that time, which took only a couple of minutes, he neither raised his face to look at me, nor did I see his face. Obviously, he knew who I was supposed to be, and for security reasons, he did not want to see me or allowed me to see him.

I finally had a legal identification. I am not a stranger or an American GI, I am an ordinary Salonica citizen now!

Having terminated the serenades at my window, playing the accordion with the girls singing, my landlady increased her affection toward me and she also asked me why not allow her to help me in my business. I told her I did not need any help, but that she was extremely helpful and pleasing during the time I was home. It would not be safe for either of us to know where I was spending many hours every day since I hadn't told her where my business was located. She did not insist, but the following day, I realized after we had breakfast that she was ready to go out.

I suspected she was going to follow me, so I hid myself in the following street and I caught her trying to follow me. I stopped her and told her that if she does this again I would leave her house. Afterwards, she never tried to follow me again. The reason I did not want her to know where the factory was located was obvious. If the German or Greek police asked about me, and Sultanitsa was home, she might deliver them to me while delivering a message. The only time my landlady found out who I was, was when the Americans came to Salonica two months after the war was over. All the other times, close to nine months, Sultanitsa, her family, and all the neighbors knew me as a progressive young businessman who came from somewhere unknown and had big plans for the future. And naturally, an ideal future husband for all the young girls of the neighborhood since I was providing money for the entire family to buy food and other needs. I was considered as a present from God though they did not know, that everyone in that house was sitting on a powder keg with an American soldier with them. If the Gestapo knew that, they might dynamite the entire neighborhood in order to kill one American spy.

Having heard warnings again and again from Yiapitzoglou and Oreopoulos that I should be more careful, I slowly began to realize that I was not really on vacation, but in a temporarily assigned period of adversity, which could be reversed unexpectedly. "How would I know?" I said, "if the Germans are looking for me right now or if they were able to find out where I live and are waiting for me at the house?" So, every time I was coming home, I would stop at the corner of the block and make sure the wives were at their doors, gossiping as usual in which things were normal. If, on the other hand, nobody was on the street, I would not go home. Instead, I would go to the "safe" house. That house, by the way, was my third, which could be used to stay overnight if I needed to or go to, or to notify members of the organization that I needed help to get out from the city in case the German Gestapo had raided the factory or the house.

I was similarly careful entering the factory. How would I know that while I was walking into the factory yard I would not find the German Gestapo waiting for me? Needing another set of eyes to keep watch over the factory while we were not there, I used Ms. Eleni, whom we had let occupy the two-room corner apartment, for that purpose. Her apartment had two large windows facing the street, which had window blinds, closed all the time so that anyone from the outside could not look inside her apartment. Since she was obliged to us for letting her stay there, I wanted her to warn me in case the Germans came in the factory looking for me. I began by convincing her of the difficulty I faced running a thriving business, especially with many jealous merchants, including the Germans, who would have liked to see us go bankrupt. She responded that she would do anything to help my business succeed. So I asked her to keep an eye out for any suspicious people, police, or Germans near or in the factory. And if she did, to tell them to wait a few minutes, that I will be arriving shortly. I told her, if she sees these people or Germans waiting for me, to open both window blinds facing the street. "Very smart," Mrs. Eleni said. "I will open both blinds immediately when I see strange people or Germans looking for you. After all, I am thankful to you for all you've done for me."

"By the way, Mrs. Eleni," I said, "would you like some olive oil or petroleum for your lamp?"

"No, my boy," she said. "I don't see many customers coming, and I feel sorry. You are wasting your father's money for nothing. I don't want anything, but if I see your business pick up, then maybe I will ask you for something."

Poor Mrs. Eleni, I said to myself, she does not know that she is right in harms way, and if that terrible day ever comes when the Germans raid us, Mrs. Eleni's apartment and herself might be the first to be blown.

After the Allied invasion in France, the war became very fierce; and the Germans began leaving gradually every day. Salonica became their embarkation post before re-directing to various war fronts. They were using trains, airplanes, even donkeys, and mules to transport their heavy armaments. OSS in Cairo had requested detailed description of all these German departures, so I was very busy collecting information, forming and coding telegrams, and sending two in the morning and two in the afternoon. Realizing that the Germans were busy scheduling troop departures that I thought they had no time to search for my wireless signals. I stopped worrying about their triangulation instruments which was wrong. I had underestimated the Gestapo's plans for finding me, and my neglect to recognize their searching ability, almost cost me my life in the coming weeks.

Though OSS Cairo was getting my messages, telling them of daily German departures, a few hundred leaving by cars or one thousand soldiers leaving by train, the big brass were not willing to send airplanes to kill a few hundred Germans, so they asked me to inform them of the big departures; **and one day we hit the jackpot.**

As I had mentioned, German military rule said that any house with two extra rooms plus an extra washroom was obliged to give it to the Germans for German officers to stay in. All the German officers were sleeping in civilian homes, and plain soldiers were staying in schools or factory buildings. From the Germans seen in the streets of the city, which sometimes seemed more than civilians, we estimated that more than fifty thousand Germans might have resided in Salonica at one time. Those Germans, either from other parts of Greece or as resting place before or after service at various fronts, were in Salonica.

Because all the officers were living in civilian's homes all over the city, it was natural if a young officer staying in a civilian house might become friendly with girls living or visiting the house the officer was staying in.

One such Greek girl, named Katerina, had become very friendly with a young German lieutenant who escorted the girl every Saturday night to the German officers entertainment center. The girl's parents and her cousin Yianni, a member of our organization, objected to the girl's relationship with the handsome German officer. They told her that after the war she might be punished, and her head shaved by vengeful Greeks. Katerina, though, insisted she was doing nothing wrong and refused to terminate her friendship with the young German Lieutenant. One Saturday, the German told the girl that he would like to see her on Wednesday night to give her many things, including clothes since he was leaving on Thursday. "What?" the girl said. "Are you really leaving? Why are you leaving? Are your friends leaving? Are you leaving by car? Can I come and say good-bye to you and to your friends?"

"No!" he said, "my entire company is leaving. You cannot come and say good-bye because there will be thousands of Germans at the railroad station, and since the train leaves at three o'clock in the afternoon on Thursday, I can see you at the bar we used to go, behind the railroad station at one o'clock in the afternoon. And maybe my friends can come and say good-bye also. In the meantime, we should meet on Wednesday night. And I will bring you many things I have collected, since I cannot take them with me wherever they send me."

"OK," the girl said, "I will see you Wednesday night."

That night, Yianni, happened to go to her house, and when the girl saw him coming, she said, "OK, all of you, you don't have to worry about me anymore; my friend, the German officer, is leaving this Thursday." Yianni quickly interrupted her. He asked "Is your German friend the only one leaving Salonica?"

"No," Katerina said, "his entire company is leaving, thousands of them are leaving!"

"Where are they leaving from?" Yianni said. "Are you going to go and say good-bye to him?"
"No, he is going to leave by train, and he told me not to go there since at three o'clock in the afternoon this Thursday, there will be thousands of Germans at the railroad station, so they would not allow anyone there. Instead, we are meeting on Wednesday night and he is going to bring me many gifts."

Immediately, Yianni called Yiapitzoglou, and Yiapitzoglou called me. I prepared a message saying that, "thousands of Germans will leave Thursday at three o'clock in the afternoon at the railroad station in Salonica." That message I sent the following morning on Sunday. OSS replied at 3:00 PM, telling me to verify again if that departure is going to stay on schedule, and if it is, they will send airplanes to bomb the railroad station at 3:00 PM on Thursday.

I replied and told them that, "definitely, I will know Wednesday night when the girl will meet with the German officer again."

On Wednesday night, the girl met with the German officer; he brought her a lot of things, and they kissed good-bye though they would try to meet at 1:00 PM at the bar behind the station if it was possible. The German also promised to write or call her from his new post when possible.

Our friend Yianni on Wednesday night pretended that he had happened to be passing from Katerina's house again, and during their conversation, he asked his cousin Katerina if the Germans were really leaving the following day.

"Yes! They are leaving," she said, "as a matter of fact, I wanted to go to the station at three o'clock in the afternoon tomorrow, Thursday, to say good-bye to his friends, but they would not allow any civilians around there at the railroad station."

Yianni called Yiapitzoglou on Wednesday night, verifying the girl's statement that there would be over three thousand Germans at the railroad station at 3:00 PM on Thursday or the following day.

Yiapitzoglou called me immediately, and I prepared and coded a message Thursday morning, saying that over three thousand Germans were leaving, at 3:00 PM today, Thursday. I made an appointment to get a reply at 12:00 noon that day. At 12:00 noon on Thursday, I received a message that American planes will come as scheduled, and to be prepared.

Yiapitzoglou was so excited that morning that he had come to the factory and waited for the reply, if the Americans would be sending the airplanes or not. So when I received the message and were sure the planes were coming, we agreed that we should go to any roof and watch to see if any planes were coming.

It should be emphasized that there were only three people in the entire country of Greece who knew that American planes were coming to bomb the railroad station at 3:00 PM, and I was one of the three. The other two were Yiapitzoglou, and Katerina's cousin.

I went home and realized what I had done. I must have looked terrible, so my landlady noticed that my face looked pale; and she asked me what was wrong; was I worrying about my business, and if she could help me in any way to let her know. If she only knew what was on my mind, that because of the message I had sent, thousands of people will be killed in a few hours. I began to feel nauseous, and weak. All these young, German soldiers, in their twenties, the prime of their lives, to die so quickly.

I told her that I was just tired and needed some rest, not of course the rest she had on her mind.

At 2:30 PM, I went into the courtyard, looking for a way to climb to the roof of the one story high building to follow the air attack as Yiapitzoglou suggested. I saw that the tree we had in our courtyard was leaning toward the wall, and I figured out that I could climb onto that tree and then jump on the roof. I had to be up there before 3:00 PM. Looking to find a reason to climb the tree without raising her suspicion, I found a ball the kids were kicking, and I threw it up and got it stuck on the roof by the chimney. Then I started climbing the tree to go up to the roof. My landlady saw me and started screaming, "Helias, Helias, what are you doing? You are going to fall and hurt yourself." And she grabbed my feet and she was pulling me down, telling me to come down. I told her that by mistake, I threw the ball up there and I would like to bring it down. "No, no," she continued to say. And with her screams, the other two tenants of the adjoining apartment in the courtyard came out to see what was happening.

I was begging her to leave me alone since I looked at my watch, and it was ten minutes to three. How could I tell her that in two minutes, airplanes would be coming and the bombardment would start? At that point, I had no other alternative but I kicked her and went to the roof when I heard, "Boom, boom." The antiaircraft had started firing at the American airplanes.

Looking to the south, I saw a row of airplanes, one behind the other, coming toward Salonica Harbor. "What is happening?" everybody was telling me. "I think airplanes are coming," I told them.

As the planes were getting closer, I counted twelve medium type bombers, probably B-25's. I thought I saw four engines, but by their shape and size looked like a B-25. In the meantime, the antiaircraft firing became more intense, and to my surprise the first airplane, the leader's airplane, was directly hit and its wing separated from the airplane and two parachutes were observed to drop out.

In a couple of seconds as the airplanes were getting closer, the third airplane in line was hit, and I saw smoke coming out and four parachutes dropped out from it.

In my last message to Cairo that morning, I had suggested that they should approach the railroad station in a straight line. I told Cairo that by using this tactic, in trail formation, the planes could drop their ordinance only on their target, avoiding the civilian sectors flanking both sides of the railroad station. And I had noticed they were coming in a straight line, but obviously, they did not anticipate such fierce antiaircraft fire, so after the remaining pilots saw the two aircraft destroyed, they broke formation and spread out over the sky. They came over me, and each plane went on its own way, dropping their ordinance on the railroad and its vicinity, and in less than a minute, they were gone. Tall plumes of smoke and flames were observed in the vicinity of the railroad, so I ran quickly toward the station. Passing by the harbor area, I saw a German open truck, and seated inside were five captured pilots still strapped to their chutes. As the Germans went to capture the sixth airman, I approached the truck. There were hundreds of people around watching the American airmen and the airmen sat silent, watching the curious people.

I went close to the truck, and with a loud voice, I hollered, "Hello, there. Hi." One airman with a rank of a captain, turned and stared at me for a few seconds, and then he moved to the other end. If only he knew that it was I who sent the message that had brought them here for their capture. Their fate still haunts me.

I wanted to go to the railroad itself, and see what had happened there. When I reached that area, the Greek police and Germans would not allow anyone to come near, so I waited together with other curious people, and in about half an hour, someone, who was working for the Germans came out and said that the train was completely destroyed. All the time they were only looking to find survivors or wounded ones. They had not started taking the bodies out yet, and he said that it would take days to untangle the bodies from the destroyed train. "Must have been thousands killed," he said. Then someone else said that he had heard that over one hundred homes were destroyed or damaged, and under those houses, hundreds of civilians may have been trapped or killed. He said that he saw a dead baby hanging on the telephone wires.

I was so upset and disgusted knowing that I had sent the message that caused all the killing and destruction, and felt guilty of what I was ordered to do. And because of this message, thousands of people were killed! At that point, I left to go home, and when I reached my block, I saw my neighbor with whom I used to talk politics with often. With a happy face, he said very loudly, "Helias, Helias, you see, the Americans did not forget us after all!"

And then quietly he said, "Helias, do you agree with me that the Americans must have known that the Germans were leaving at 3:00 PM? Don't you think so?"

"Yes, they probably knew about it, but to tell you how I feel, I wish they had not known!" I said.

"I don't understand, what do you mean?" I did not reply; I just lowered my head and went inside. I felt very sad! For the first time, I cursed my job.

Up to that day, I had enjoyed being a spy; I enjoyed the thrills thinking that whatever I was doing was a game. Only that day when I saw the results of a twenty words telegram, I felt as though I dropped the bombs by myself. A single message, that took me a couple minutes to send, could be the cause of thousands to be killed hit me like a rock and I could not justify that it was my duty to have sent that telegram. I asked myself, just because we are at war, did I have the right to make thousand of families unhappy and mournful? Trying to lighten up the burden of guilt that was torturing me, I said to myself that those three thousand Germans if allowed to go to the war front, might have killed thousands of Americans. So I calmed down a little bit and I told myself that I was a soldier and I acted as a soldier. And a good soldier has no feelings in order to do his job, that I was just following orders, and I did this well.

The following day, the newspapers wrote that the "barbarian Americans" bombed our city and destroyed eighty-five homes killing 450 civilians. They did not mention how many Germans were killed but the word was around that more than 2,500 Germans were killed, bombed by American planes at the time the loaded train was ready to depart from the station.

I prepared a message to send to Cairo, notifying them that we had witnessed two airplanes shot down and a third seemed to be smoking as it was leaving southward. Also, six pilots were captured, one with the rank of captain.

When I went to the factory to send the message, I found everybody there, happy and congratulating each other. As I walked in, they all ran to me, and when they saw me sad, they asked me why? "Do you know?" I said to them, "that if the estimate was right, that with the civilians killed, our message cost the lives of three thousand people! Can I be proud of that?"

Yiapitzoglou then said that it was our duty to send that message, and that is why we had been sent here. "Those 2,500 Germans, if they went to the front might have killed, who knows, many thousands of Americans. So don't feel sorry, have a glass of Ouzo and be proud."

I should mention that as the days passed by, the girl, Katerina, who had told her cousin Yianni about the Germans leaving that day, waited in vain to get a call from the German officer. Since the train never left and the young German lieutenant never called the girl back, it was almost certain that he and all his friends must have been killed.

A few days after the bombardment, Yianni went to his cousin's house, and as soon as Katerina saw Yianni, said to him, "now you don't have to worry about me anymore, my German friend is now dead and likely all his friends too. I did not get any telephone call, so all must be dead." And Yianni noticed tears from the girl's eyes.

"By the way," she also said, "do you still think they are going to cut my hair after the war? All these Germans are dead."

"What?" Yianni said, "to cut your hair? Most likely, they will probably decorate you or make a statue of you, Katerina!"

"What are you talking about?", she said. "Why are they going to decorate me?" Then he began to tell her what had happened.

"Do you know that because of what you told me about the German departure at 3:00 PM on that Thursday was the reason that brought the American planes here?

"What?" said the girl. "You mean you told someone and the planes came? You mean, I killed everybody with my big mouth? I caused all that misery? Do you know that my friend, the German lieutenant, had gone to two universities and he knew more about Ancient Greece than both of us put together? He told me he was going to return after the war and marry me. He loved Greece. He wanted to live in Greece. He had studied Ancient Greek. He had read all the Greek tragedies and now I was his tragedy."

"Please, don't feel like this Katerina. You did not know it," Yianni told her. It was I who did it."

"Not to feel badly, not to feel sad? You tricked me!" she said. And at that time, the girl became furious, jumped on Yianni and began hitting him all over. She finally fell down crying and she suffered a nervous breakdown. She was taken to the hospital, but she recovered fast, still hoping for that telephone call that never came.

Chapter 12

- Gestapo's continuous search for the American wireless following the bombardment of the railroad station by American planes
- American spy caught in street battle between Germans and partisans
- A German lieutenant's desperate plea to avoid transfer to the Russian front reaching a member of our organization
- German trucks surrounding the block where the wireless was hidden; OSS agent able to avoid imminent capture

After the bombardment of the railroad station, the Gestapo must have concluded that an OSS team was responsible for the bombings, knowing precisely when a trainload of German troops was scheduled to leave. During one of our meetings, our discussions followed that they would be increasing their attempts to locate our cell. Yiapitzoglou suggested that we limit our communications to one daily message and to add a second watchman outside the factory.

"The Gestapo," Yiapitzoglou said, "has many tricks up their sleeves and will not stop their schemes until they find the wireless. So let us be extremely careful from now on!"

One afternoon the Germans were installing telephone wires in the street outside from the factory. The Sergeant supervising the installation realized that our factory had a lot of space which the Germans could use to store their equipment instead of hauling the tools back to the same place the next day. None of our group was there to speak with the Germans, but he spoke to Mrs. Eleni. Mrs. Eleni did not understand what the Germans were trying to say, and while they brought the tools into the yard, Mrs. Eleni raised all the window blinds, to warn me as we had agreed upon. As I was returning, I saw the blinds open and I immediately assumed the Germans were in the factory. Instead of going towards the factory gates I turned and walked in the opposite direction and waited for the rest of the group. I had arrived half an hour before my next transmission and I was sure they had not arrived yet. As soon as I spotted them coming I signaled at them not to go to the factory since we may have German visitors waiting for us. Nikitas told me that he would go check out the situation at the factory, and see if the shutters were still open. He saw the sergeant coming out from the gate wearing his tool belt. While he was waiting to see if any more Germans were in the factory yard, Mrs. Eleni began closing the window shutters. He returned and told me that he did not think the Germans were from the secret police judging from his tool belt and demeanor. We both walked carefully towards the gate and since the shutters were closed we knew there wasn't anyone left on the factory grounds. We entered the factory and Mrs. Eleni told me that a German had left his tools in the yard which prompted her to open the window shutters. I thanked her and told her to continue the same protocol every time the Germans, or someone suspicious, is waiting by the factory.

The German sergeant came to pick up his equipment the following day, and explained to me that he would be working in that neighborhood for about ten days. He asked if it was possible to continue storing his heavy tools when he is not working. I immediately told him that I had no objection. As a matter of fact, I could not deny his request, but as a result our group became good friends with the sergeant, who was from Austria and never liked the war. At 4 pm, quitting time, he would leave his tools and then talk to us for thirty minutes every day.

He was an extremely friendly individual and conversed quite freely in German to his liking. Perhaps he also liked my conversations, or maybe he wanted to strike up a friendship. After quitting time, he particularly loved to talk about Greek mythology, history, and the war. One day, I had an appointment at 1630 hours. The sergeant loved our company so that he did not wish to leave. At 1620 hours, Oreopoulos pointed to his watch and gestured with his index finger. It was time to assemble the wireless. I understood what he meant and thought of a way to interrupt his stay. I got up and told the sergeant that I had other appointments but that I was thirsty, and some water would quench my thirst first, thinking that he would excuse himself at this time and leave. As I stood up, he also got up and he began to walk toward the front gate while I walked toward the inner room's door. Unbeknownst to me, the sergeant began to collect his tools, which were next to the front gate and decided to return for a drink of water. And as I was beginning to connect my radio to a wire that was concealed behind my desk, (which in turn was connected to the main antenna in the factory), the German returned to enter the outer room. While the sergeant began to open the outer room's glass door, Stavros quickly jumped on him from behind, knocking him to the ground with Stavros falling on top of the unwary and now confused German. At this very moment, I had put my headphones on, when to my great surprise, I heard the calamity. I jumped up from my chair and went into the outer room, closing the door to the inner room behind me. There I saw Stavros on top of the sergeant and asked politely, "What happened in here, Stavros?" The German said, "I also wanted some water and wanted to go inside the room to get it." Stavros began apologizing to him and repeatedly said in Greek, "I tripped and fell on him. And if he wanted water he should have told me and I would have brought it to him." Regardless, in the confusion, we all apologized to each other including the German. He left without any one of us being certain that he had not seen anything.

When Yiapitzoglou returned that evening, we told him about the incident. I saw the anger in his reddened face; he could not believe that we had started assembling the wireless while the German was still on the premises. "Never do that again," he said. "Let us lose our appointment to transmit instead of being caught because of our stupidity." "If there is a German near our place, we should not dare bring the wireless out from the hiding place," he said. And we all agreed to comply with that request. Using the wireless had become such a routine that we were neglecting these unsecured premises in which I was operating the wireless. It was so unfit and dangerous that we were lucky we had not been discovered at any time during the nine month period we were there, and I was operating the wireless in a room with a glass door, big windows and an unlocked door. Anybody coming into the factory would have seen me with my headphones on. I guess it was my naivete and youth.

Yiapitzoglou, though, who was twenty-five years my senior and more mature, then said, "to be caught by triangulation instruments we could not condemn ourselves, but to be caught because we did not want to lose an appointment, we could never forgive ourselves."

I left the factory that day and I had so many things on my mind that I wanted to walk, so I walked past St. Demetrios Church, the biggest church in the city. There were beggars on each side of the street, in front of the church, sitting or lying on the street with dirty clothes, stretching their hands for someone to give them something. I gave all of them some money, and as I was leaving, I saw an old woman that grabbed my attention. Her clothes were clean, and she had such a sad face that looked like the Virgin Mary looking at her son, Jesus, on the cross, crucified. I asked myself what misfortune had happened to this woman, that she was forced to come here and beg. She reminded me of my blind grandmother who most of the time wore a sad expression not being able to see the world. As if I knew that lady well, I put my hand in my pocket, which was full of money, and took a big pack of big bills and put them in the woman's hand. The woman, without looking at them turned, and in a low toned voice, said to me, "Bless you my son and let God be with you and protect you wherever you are."

"I thank you, and God bless you and help you also," I told her. I left before the other beggars saw what I had given her.

As I was going home, I followed a different route that I usually used, and I realized that though it was not late, there was nobody in the streets. "What is happening?" I was saying to myself, when I heard a pistol shot and saw in a nearby window someone signaling me to come near. He told me that Germans were firing at the partisans who were in a house across the street and that I was caught in a crossfire. "Where can I go," I said. And the man said that the janitor of that apartment house had locked the entrance door but a little bit down and across the street was an overnight drugstore, and they have their door open, so he told me to go there. I saw where the drugstore was and tried to cross, and by mistake, I hit a garbage can and it started rolling in the middle of the street. The Germans saw something moving and they were firing at it with bullets, and the garbage can jumped and hit the sidewalks on both sides, making a tremendous noise. With that noise, I heard people coming toward me, so I ran across the street and saw someone opening the door for me to come in. Since I realized that in a few minutes, the Germans would come to the drugstore searching for partisans, I asked the store owner if there was a rear exit for me to leave. "Yes, there is," he said. "But why leave? The Germans are looking for partisans only. You don't have to worry if you have an identification."

Thinking that the Germans may give me a thorough examination and trying to avoid this, I left from the rear door, and finally, I went home. While I was going, I thought that I could have been killed in that crossfire, and if I was killed, the organization and everybody else who knew me would think that the Gestapo or some other organization traced me down and killed me. What irony, again I thought, to have been saved so many times just to get killed because I went down a different street. When I entered the house, my landlady saw me very upset and asked me what happened. I told her that I had left my work; I had passed St. Demetrios Church and I had seen a beggar woman that I had given money, and that accidentally, I had fallen in a crossfire between the partisans and Germans; and I was almost shot.

She listened to me very attentively, and at the end, said that the old beggar must have been the Virgin Mary; and she was testing you, if you were a good man. By your mercy, she gave you protection and saved you. I did not say anything; I listened to her and I really wanted to believe her.

After the bombardment of the railroad station, which OSS in Cairo considered a great achievement despite the loss of three planes, they continued reminding me to inform them if another massive departure was to take place. Obviously, the Germans did not want to try a similar exodus, so they were noticed to be sending soldiers by airplanes or by truck convoys. They knew that an American underground organization must exist in Salonica; and we were sure that the Gestapo would not stop unless they caught us.

As mentioned before, our organization had members to provide us with information not only in the harbor, airports, railroads, and other areas, but also, we had members in German offices: people who swept the floors and cleaned the toilets. Though we had a few people who were working directly in German offices, only one man named Spyros was working in an important building, the HQ of Gestapo. Spyros's job as a janitor was crucial to us. He cleaned toilets in a very well-guarded area of the Gestapo's HQ and we were sure that information on the railroad bombing and a possible underground cell in Salonica must be in the Gestapo's headquarters, where Spyros worked. Spyros told us that in the building's garage, there were many trucks, which had triangulation equipment on them. Since Spyros was going in those buildings only after 5:00 PM, he was not able to know what those trucks were doing during the day, the time we were using the wireless. During the time Spyros was cleaning the place, there was a guard watching him, so he could not steal or read any daily schedules or actions. However, the only valuable information we did get from Spyros was about any hostages or prisoners.

OSS office in Cairo was also interested in ship departures, and especially, they were interested in an Italian mine-laying ship, which was docked in Salonica Harbor; and we were repeatedly told to let them know when the ship was preparing to leave Salonica Harbor so that they can destroy it. Our friends who were working in the harbor area were to inform us when the ship was getting ready to leave.

The day had come and we got two or three notifications that the ship was getting loaded with provisions, so we were sure the ship was going to leave within a couple of days. That day was Tuesday, and we estimated that the ship should leave by the next Thursday. I notified Cairo that the ship they wanted to sink was getting provisions and that we expect it to depart by next Thursday. "Good news," they told me from OSS headquarters, "Good job, Cando, keep up the good work." That was the last sentence of their latest message. In the meantime, in September 1944, the Allies were pushing the Germans on all fronts; so the Germans were pulling back almost all their troops from Greece. Hundreds of thousands of Germans had died the previous winter in Russia, so the Russians had pushed the Germans almost to their borders. Everyone by that time knew that the Germans had lost the war, even the Germans understood they would soon be defeated. The German sergeant who was leaving his tools at the factory used to talk with me, since I understood a lot of German and since we had become friends and by sitting with him after working hours and drinking wine, he had told me that as the war was developing they had lost the war. He would hate to leave Greece, especially if he was going to Russia. "If the war ended," he said. "I would like to go back to Austria, but if it happened and I was forced to become a prisoner, I would not mind to be prisoner with the American army or English army. I would not like to become a prisoner with the Russian army. They will kill us all!" the sergeant said. He was actually Austrian, not German. "We Austrians were forced to become German soldiers. We had no choice," the sergeant said.

Going back to the German Gestapo's office where Spyros was working, we were smart to see in time that a big scheme was prearranged in order to trick us, and finally be caught. Fortunately, though, an unknown power protected us and directed the enemy to change plans and look for a strange, but more favorable solution for us.

On Wednesday, a day before the Italian ship was scheduled to leave the Harbor of Salonica, Spyros went to work, as usual, at five o'clock at night to start cleaning. Inside the building, he saw that the lieutenant in the head office was still in when usually the building would be empty except for the guards. He started collecting the wastebaskets in the main room accompanied continuously by a guard. And when he reached the lieutenant's office, the lieutenant told the guard to leave, since he said to the guard, he would watch him clean his room. When the guard left, the lieutenant closed the door and told Spyros to sit down!

Spyros sat down not knowing what the lieutenant was planning to do, but in the meantime, he felt chills all over his body.

"Listen carefully, Spyros, and don't be afraid. I know that you belong to an organization. It must be an American that sent information and bombed our train a few weeks ago."

Spyros did not let the lieutenant continue; he became yellow and told the lieutenant he did not know what he was talking about. He did not belong to any organization.

Truthfully enough, Spyros never belonged to any organization, only his friend Jim who was a member of our organization. Jim had approached Spyros and told him that there is a patriotic organization; he did not tell him which one it was, if it was American or English or Greek, and suggested to him

---

(Despite the fact that it sounds impossible or unorthodox and difficult to believe it is true. The reader has to believe that during the war, the time at which everybody's life depended on a fast decision or miscalculated judgment, we could expect all types of actions. By reading the following, decide what you would have done yourselves, German or civilian, in order to save your life.)

to be observant of any prisoners or hostages, and to let Jim know. Jim and Spyros would meet weekly in a nearby park to discuss details.

The lieutenant repeated to him that they knew he was involved with some organization, but he told him not to worry about it. Again, Spyros denied everything, thinking that it could be a trick. But the lieutenant stopped him and told him that he should not worry, that unless he listened, he would show his file and pictures the Gestapo had taken of him together with someone else, the someone else being Jim at the park. "Spyros," the lieutenant said, "even if you belonged to an organization we have concluded that, obviously you were not very active or important. We determined that when we had left important documents purposely unprotected, and you did not even look at them or copy them or steal them. So you don't have to worry, just listen to what I have to say." Spyros at that point calmed down and told the lieutenant to continue, who surprisingly enough, was speaking in half way descent Greek! The lieutenant, then with a sad expression started saying that the war on all the fronts was not being won, and they would lose the war. "Before the war is finished, though, very soon, Germans will leave Greece and all of us will be sent to other fronts, which need immediate reinforcement, which unfortunately right now is the Russian front. And it is likely that most of us in Greece will be sent there. If I was sent there, and the war ended with me being a prisoner in Russian hands I would be killed. If they don't kill us, for sure they would torture me for many years so, do you see what I'm telling you? I really am Austrian and half German so I propose to you the following. Since, I know for sure, that our department is very close to capturing the American radio which, we know is operating in the Agia Triada area, I want to help you not to be caught if you help me now. So, do what I am going to tell you."

"This Thursday, they have ordered that all German radios not be operating so that they could easily spot your radio, and locate its position. And by using other tricks, we expect for sure the American radio will be sending messages this Thursday, which would make the capture very promising. So for your own good don't operate this Thursday and also it would be better to move far from the area of Agia Triada since they will concentrate their search in that area."

"Now, Spyros," the German Lieutenant said, "You are asking yourself, why am I telling you all these secrets?"

"The reason is that, besides speaking Greek, I also speak a little Russian, so most likely, they will send me to Russian front. We are getting ready to leave Greece, so before I leave I am trying to help you not to get caught, and in exchange I would like for you to help me."

"The day I am to leave Salonica, I would like to surrender to your organization and be taken prisoner by the Americans. I think being a prisoner with the Americans would not be such a bad situation after all. After this Thursday, after the triangulation groups will be all around you, and of course, you trust me now and tell the proper man not to operate the wireless this Thursday, and after you are assured of my sincerity, then I would like to meet someone of your group, or someone communicates with me, and assures me that you are willing to accept me as a prisoner of the American forces at the proper time."

Spyros was listening very carefully and could not really believe what he was hearing all that time. Was it really true that the German was that much disgusted with the war that he wanted to become an American prisoner? Spyros was still careful not to accept what he had heard, not knowing if the lieutenant was using a trick to make him accept, and for that, Spyros kept silent.

The lieutenant understood that, and he told him to go and finish what he was supposed to do, and then leave and go and tell the organization of what he had told him. And that he wanted to hear if the organization was willing to believe him and agree to fulfill his wish to be taken prisoner.

Spyros got up but still trembling all over. He got out from the room and met with the guard in order to continue cleaning the various offices. After he had finished, he left and he went straight to Jim's house, the friend who had involved him with the organization, which organization to that day was unknown to him. Jim had told him it was a patriotic organization, and now he had found out it could be the Americans. "I will kill that Jim," Spyros said to himself as he was going to meet him. When he reached his house, he found him having supper with his wife, and when they saw Spyros, they invited him to sit down and have a drink with them, which he said he needed. Spyros then told Jim that he, should pour himself a drink, which, he would need after he hears what he was about to tell him. After they had eaten, Spyros told Jim to go for a walk outside, and when they were not too far from the house, Spyros turned to Jim and said, "you son of a bitch, why the hell didn't you tell me that you were working for American spies? Did I have to find it out the hard way?" Spyros said.

"What is the difference what organization we are working for? All the organizations work against the enemy, but let us get this straight," Jim said. "Who told you that the organization is American, and for your information, it is American!"

"Oh, it is the Americans." Spyros said. "I was told about it by the Germans and specifically from an officer of the Gestapo."

When Jim heard that he started laughing, thinking that Spyros was joking!

"Come now, Spyros, tell me, how did you find out it is the Americans?" Jim said.

"Look, Jim," Spyros said, "I only had one drink. I am not drunk. I am telling you the truth! I know, you think this is a joke, but it is the truth. A German lieutenant told me."

Spyros started from the beginning, telling him exactly what happened; and that the German told Jim what plans they have in mind to trick the American radio group and finally find the location of the wireless, and also what the lieutenant wished for: to be taken as an American prisoner.

Jim could hardly believe his ears, but looking at Spyros' fearful disposition, he had to believe him. That night, Jim called Yiapitzoglou who also could not believe what Jim was telling him.

Next morning, Yiapitzoglou called me and Nicos Oreopoulos to meet him at the factory, and he told us what Jim had told him. We all believed that the Germans knew more about our location than we knew but we were completely surprised to hear what the German said to Spyros. For the first time, we came to believe that our end was coming very soon. "First of all, they said they know we are operating in Agia Triada," we said, "which is true, we are in Agia Triada."

"Second, they know we are going to be on the air on Thursday, since the Italian mine-laying ship is most likely leaving on Thursday." "It is not difficult to understand," I said, "why they chose Thursday to forbid all the German radios to operate: so that they catch us!" Of what the German lieutenant said, we concluded that Thursday was set by the Germans to finally locate us and invade the factory. But they didn't know who, or where.

"Our first concern," Yiapitzoglou said, "is to save ourselves. We should believe what the lieutenant recommended and not operate the wireless on Thursday, not even go to the factory at all! Watch for any trucks that circulate around here for a couple of days, starting today, Wednesday afternoon till this Sunday, and then we see what we can do later. Let us see if the German is telling us the truth. The triangulation trucks should be all around Agia Triada on Thursday."

I stopped and I reminded him that OSS in Cairo had reminded us many times not to miss sending them the departure day of the Italian ship.

"Don't you see, Helias," Yiapitzoglou said, "that the Germans are putting the departure of the Italian ship as bait? Do you want to use the wireless on Thursday and satisfy the Germans by locating you? I am not coming here to the factory," Yiapitzoglou said. "Neither you nor anybody. Since you really want to send a message about the ship's departure, send it this afternoon, not tomorrow."

"But the ship has not left the harbor yet, and suppose it does not leave at all," I said. "Do you want the Americans to send airplanes to sink the ship if it not left yet, and endanger the lives of many people for nothing?"

"First of all, we wait till tomorrow morning," I said. "We'll find out if the ship is really leaving, and when our guys tell us the ship is going out the harbor, I will make a short message and I will try to send it as soon as possible, tomorrow morning."

"I cannot stop you of doing your duty; after all, you are a soldier and you think as a soldier. But I still tell you, you are endangering yourself and might be caught. Don't forget, a heroic decision can make you a dead hero," Yiapitzoglou said.

In the meantime, Nicos Oreopoulos, who was listening all the time, saying nothing, told me that if I had to come to the factory he would inform the two watchmen to come and warn them to be extra cautious of the anticipated danger that was expected to come. I told Oreopoulos that I would be in the factory 8:30AM, and if the ship was not leaving the harbor, I would not send anything at the scheduled time of 9:15 AM I had established previously with Cairo.

As we were leaving the factory, Yiapitzoglou turned to me again and told me to think twice before I decide to operate the wireless on Thursday. "Everything indicates," Yiapitzoglou said, "that we have been set up to be tricked to be on the air, and you're falling for it!"

"Think of yourself just once." he told me. "The German is willing to become a prisoner when he sees there is no better solution to save his life," Yiapitzoglou said, and then he squeezed my hand, and we all left to go home. The following morning, Thursday, I was at the factory at 8:20 AM and found Oreopoulos there and the two watchmen. I was told that our men in the harbor area, who were following the ship's departure, called Oreopoulos and told him that the ship was lifting its anchors; and Oreopoulos felt that while they were talking, the ship would probably be out of the harbor. I thanked Oreopoulos for the information, and I told him that I had plenty of time to write the coded message and be ready by 9:15 AM, our next appointment with Cairo. I told him to leave; he was not needed there anymore; why endanger himself in case the Germans invaded the place? Then I called the two watchmen and warned them to be extremely alert and if they noticed anything strange to run to me and tell me. I told them my life may depend entirely on their alertness. If they saw the Germans running towards the factory, they should run faster to notify me so that I can try to escape. They both told me that they would never abandon me; I believed them and they left for their posts, one cutting wood in the front, the other walking around the block. Both guards were holding guns as usual. I sat down and coded the message about the Italian ship leaving the harbor, as short as I could, only twenty words, the smallest permitted, each word five letters. At 9:00 AM, I set up the wireless and I was ready at exactly 9:15 AM when I heard Cairo call, "Cando, Cando." I answered back and told him I had an urgent message for him and gave a special signal that it was extremely dangerous sending this message, and I instructed Cairo not to interrupt.

I started sending the message and I had not gone more that three quarters through when I heard someone talking in the courtyard. Then the door opened up and Nikitas, the watchman whose job was to patrol around the block, jumped into the room. He threw the gun on my table, and screaming, he said to me, *"the German trucks have surrounded the block, in*

two minutes they will be here, get out to save your life and run out toward the exit." The other watchman, who was by the gate, saw Nikitas running out; he came and dropped his gun and also ran out, leaving me with my headphones still on while Cairo, not knowing what was happening, was signaling me to continue with the telegram. I signaled the operator in Cairo to change frequency, and when he came back to me at the other frequency, I finished. I did not know where I found the courage to continue sending that message, for I can still recall how close the trucks were when I finally finished, even though my ears were covered with the headphones.

Having finished the telegram, I refused to accept their message; Cairo was signaling for me to accept. Taking my headphones off for a couple of seconds, I stood, not knowing what to do; on the table sat the wireless, one .45 caliber gun, the two guns the watchmen dropped and a box with two grenades. "Should I try to hide all of these," I said to myself, "or why don't I just try to escape as fast as possible and let them find them; anyway, if they had found the exact house, they should expect to find a wireless." So I put two grenades in my pocket, thinking that if at any moment the Germans might pounce on me, and by throwing the grenades at them during that confusion, I could push out the window, which led to the house where the German officers lived, and go out from their yard gate, leaving from another street. So with the two grenades in my pocket and the .45 caliber gun in my hand, I walked toward our yard's exit. Looking through the iron gate, I did not see Germans at the ready; I only saw people walking and laughing not knowing, of course, what was going on. So I thought to go out and mix in with them and be one of them. But what about the gun I was holding and the two grenades in my pockets? I said I must go back and drop them in the hiding area. When I went inside the room and saw the wireless still connected with the battery on the table and the guns next to it I decided to disconnect the wireless, throw it and everything in the hiding place, and then go back and walk out. I did that; I threw the gun I was holding and the two grenades in the hiding place as well, and without holding anything, I went out from the gate, hoping to see people walking and laughing as I did before.

Instead, to my surprise, I heard soldiers running with high boots and German voices hollering very loudly, "Raus! Raus!" and others ordering commands toward the civilians. With a fast look in the direction of the street where the noise was coming from, I saw two Germans from the right running toward the direction I was in, followed by a small German car with more Germans on it.

My god, I said to myself, *they are coming for me; they must have located our wireless. It is too late to run out in the street from this exit. I must try to escape from the back way.* How stupid of me not to have left before when I had the chance, even with the gun and the hand grenades on me, I could have mixed with the other civilians and leave. Now I was trapped in here with nothing to defend myself with. My only chance to escape is toward the window that led to the house where the German officers stayed.

Hearing the Germans coming closer and anticipating the worst, I directed myself from the gate towards the room, where I kept the wireless. By passing next to the hiding place I thought of arming myself with the .45 and the two grenades, but since the sound of the running Germans was getting close to our gate I decided not to lose any more time and try to escape. I heard our gate open, and as I turned to face the gate, I heard a shot and saw a civilian running inside our yard, chased by two German policemen. The civilian, instead of coming inside our building, was running towards the long end of our yard where there was a low wall behind which was another yard of our neighbor's house. Obviously, the man knew of the low wall and he tried to reach the wall but as he tried to jump over, I heard another shot. I didn't see what happened next. I had no time to find out if they had killed the man or captured him, I just did not want the Germans to come inside the factory or find me.

Up to that moment I did not know if the German police had surrounded the block as Nikitas had told me, and if they were chasing the wrong man. Was this an independent incident, I asked myself, that just happened the same time the Gestapo was after me?

The reality was that the German police was in our yard, they had fired twice at someone and I should expect them to enter our premises any moment to find me.

I said to myself, "I should get out of here one way or another". Going into the yard where the Germans stood would be stupid. The most logical exit was to jump from the rear window into the yard where the German officers resided. By that time, the Germans had seized the chased individual and they were coming towards the entrance of the building where I was. I had no time to lose, I had to jump out before the Germans came inside.I went to my escape window. Just as I was ready to kick out the window frame, I thought to wait for a moment in case a German policeman saw me. Since the Germans had not entered the building yet, why not open the window and jump out, without kicking it? I did that, but because the window frame was loosely held on the wall, as I tried to go through the window, I pushed the frame with the entire window and fell into the garden of the adjoining house. The noise was so loud but fortunately neither the homeowner or the residing Germans were at home. By going through the garden of that house I left from the exit gate that led me to another side street, and I was able to mix in with the other pedestrians. I was relieved, and thanked God that I was not caught by the Germans. Lucky again!

I asked myself whether the incident with the Germans chasing that man was related to the search for my radio? Did they think they had found the American agent when they were chasing that other man? Or was the other man an isolated case? While there were chasing him he must have known that going through our yard and jumping the rear wall was a good escape route, and that is why he opened our gate, running towards our yard when the Germans fired the first shot. And as he ran towards the rear wall, that is where the Germans fired the second shot. I almost felt like telling the chasing Germans that you're after the wrong man: it is ME you are after, not him! From a distance of about two hundred feet I glanced carefully at our entrance. I was trying to spot the trucks that Nikitas said surrounded the neighborhood.

Though I should have been careful to try and get away from our block, I become curious, which took me closer to the factory. When I approached the entrance I saw that the gate was still opened. Next to the gate there was a police car and a civilian sitting inside, and I recognized this man to be a neighbor living two houses across the street. Standing next to the car was one German policeman. I passed by unnoticed by my neighbor. He was about fifty years old and I assumed he must have been involved in some organization. His name and address may have been given to the German police. So when he heard the German police coming he tried to escape and our yard presented a good escape route because it was deep and if he ran to the end and jumped the low wall he could escape to the next block. When I saw the Germans chasing him in our yard and I heard the two shots, I thought he was killed. But he was alive, sitting inside the German car; either they missed him or they fired to make him surrender. I was sure then that the Germans were only after that man and not after me. That is why they did not come inside the office I was in first.

I wanted to find where the trucks were, as Nikitas said. So I went to the corner and there, to my surprise, I saw the big truck.

The canvas on the back was pulled to the side diagonally, and I could clearly see three Germans, seated on each side of the truck and in the front, two Germans operating two triangulation units with their antennas turning continuously around. I walked to the other two corners of the block and saw similar trucks, trying to locate my wireless's signals. As the German had told Spyros, they knew I was working in Agia Triada; so they must have been hiding in some nearby street Thursday morning, waiting for me to notify Cairo about the Italian ship's departure. Since they had ordered all German radios to be silent that morning, it would be a piece of cake to find me. I could only thank Nikita's quick action to inform me, and the switching of frequencies that saved my skin.

In Cairo, during my training, they had told us that I should not expect the Gestapo to be on the street searching for me. "After they find the general area your radio is operating, they will hide their instruments in houses. Then your goose will be cooked." Fortunately, other factors also came into play: the numerous homes in this predominantly residential area, and the brevity of the message.

I was curious to see how long would the trucks with the triangulation units remain at the three corners of the block? I sat down on a sidewalk cafe and watched the faces of two Gestapo officers, standing outside from one of the three trucks, how let down and disappointed they were that they had come so close to catching us and failed. In the meantime, two other Germans inside the truck were turning the antennas of the triangulation units in all directions, trying to locate my signal, which had ceased a long time ago.

I wanted to tell them that I was watching their suffering and I was enjoying their failure. For three more hours, they waited in vain to intercept my signals, while I sat, sipping one coffee after another, staring at their disappointed faces. If I was caught as a prisoner, I should expect plenty of torture by the Gestapo to learn the names of my associates. And in my special case, when they found out that I was an American soldier, my tortures would have been more numerous and more severe. If I ever had to face those unfortunate circumstances, I would have utilized the poison capsule, the Q pill, which I always had hidden on me, in the lining of my jacket.

Thinking about all these things that could have happened, made me realize that I should be thanking God that I am still alive. Maybe I should visit the St. Demetrios Church again and see if that lady I had given money to is still there, who had blessed me with "thank you my boy and let God be with you wherever you go!"

After waiting for more than three hours, finally the trucks left, still circling the area one last time. At that moment, I thought of the German whose warning had saved me. *Without his warning, I would have been caught for sure.* I remembered the times I was sending two or even three coded messages at the same time, and if I had not been warned, I would probably have sent at least one more message about the departing Italian ship and had received at least one message in which case I would have stayed on the air longer. Yes, I said to myself, that German was telling us the truth. I believe him now, that he tried to help us and he did. He had saved my life and we should try to inform Cairo about him and try to hold him when the proper time comes. As a matter of fact, I said to myself, I wish I could go to him and secretly tell him how grateful I am of his help.

That evening, we all met at a restaurant and embraced each other, all grateful that we all were OK. Yiapitzoglou squeezed my shoulders and tried to show me how happy he was that I had not been caught. "I told you," he said, "not to go and that we should have listened to the German but you put your duty first; now let us drink to us!" Then Nikitas came to me and asked me to excuse him for running out and leaving me alone after he had come and notified me that the Germans had surrounded the block. "I got so scared," he said, "that I ran out without even asking you," he said, "if you wanted help to hide the guns and wireless." Nikitas looked upset.

I told Nikitas he had done what he was supposed to do. "You did that," I told him. If you stayed inside while the Germans came in, you would get killed for nothing. It was me and my radio they were after, not you. Your warning saved me." Nikitas felt better.

Then Nicos Oreopoulos's turn came to talk and he said that he should not have left either. "Helias, I thought that if they caught and tortured you, you would tell them about me. Where would my family and I hide? All of Salonica knows me, and I thought I needed to flee Salonica. I am sorry."

"I know you are a well-known merchant in Salonica and your name would never be revealed by me. Before the torturer's hand would touch me I would break a poison pill and end my life, and nothing would ever be said."

Yiapitzoglou interrupted me at that point as if he did not want to think that I would take my own life, so we filled up our glasses of wine, toasted one another with happy wishes for each other. Yiapitzoglou suggested that we don't send any messages till we were sure they had stopped looking for us.

At that point, I referred to the German who helped us survive. "Does any one of you," I said, "think that the German is waiting to hear of our appreciation of his warnings that led to our survival?"

Interestingly enough, everyone looked at each other and no one had a suggestion.

Since no one had any suggestions, I turned to them and said "I thought it would be the proper thing to do by going to Gestapo HQ, introduce ourselves, and say . . . 'We are, Cosmas Yiapitzoglou, a trusted representative of the OSS in Salonica, Helias Nicolaou, corporal of the U.S. Army in the Middle East and a member of the OSS, and guards, Nicos, Nikitas, and Stavros.

"Firstly, Lieutenant, we would like to thank you for notifying us on the German plans of seizing our wireless, and because of that, we are informing you that we are at your service to accept you as a prisoner whenever you wish." We all laughed, and then Yiapitzoglou suggested that since I was the only American soldier and since the lieutenant wanted to be a prisoner of the American army, it should be proper that I should go by myself only, not with anybody else, and offer him my willingness to accept him as a prisoner anytime he is available. We laughed again to that second suggestion, and then we all became quiet. "Truthfully," I said to them, "I think eventually we have to think about him, after all he saved my life and we are here, happy as we are, enjoying ourselves instead of preparing a funeral. I don't think we should make a decision tonight, but let us not exclude the possibility of helping him. If we hear months from now that the Russians killed all the prisoners they caught, would you feel better, knowing that at least one has been saved by us?"

At that point, Oreopoulos stopped us from talking about the German. With a few words, he said that we should forget about the German. "It would be impossible to communicate with a Gestapo member, and if he is expecting any help from us, he is stupid to think that members of our organization would endanger themselves to help him become a prisoner. On the other hand, he may be very smart by trying new ways to trick us to his game of German trickery. Don't forget he is a Gestapo man, and Gestapo men are fanatical." With those words, we left to go home, but before we left, Yiapitzoglou told us that Spyros, the janitor left his job, took his family and left Salonica for Yianena, a city miles away.

Spyros's disappearance must have enraged the lieutenant, so we agreed that we should wait for a couple weeks before we try to send anymore messages again in that location. "Cairo must think that we have been chased by the Gestapo, or maybe they think the worst, that we may have been caught by not keeping up with the scheduled appointments, especially from the tone of my last message."

We all left the restaurant, and when I went home, I saw Annoula waiting for me at her door. "Oh my god," I said, "I hope she is not planning another singing serenade with her friends in the state I am in." She complained to me that I was avoiding her and that she is very fond of me and that she would like to go out on a date again if I did not mind. At that point, her parents came out, the father being a professor at the University of Salonica, and since I had been approved as a future son-in-law by the entire family, they themselves invited me to have a supper with them. I accepted, thinking that being with a family would take my mind away from the recent escape. If they only knew what their prospective son-in-law was and in what dangerous business he was involved in, they would forbid their daughter to talk to me and move away from that neighborhood till the end of the war.

While eating, the professor reminded me the day I had taken them to the theater and had found us tickets the last moment. "I still cannot forget," the professor said, "how you managed to get the best seats at the 'sold out' premiere." I laughed while he continuously said, "when everybody, including the actors stared at us, like we were dignitaries."

"Well," I said, "I have good friends in high places."

That evening, I found it difficult trying to find answers to questions like where I came from, how did I become so successful at that age, and others, but at the end, I think I managed to avoid suspicion even from this very smart professor of mathematics.

At the end, when I found a chance to be alone with Annoula, a warm kiss made me to forget completely what had happened in the last few days of terror.

———————

As the time passed, we saw more and more Germans leaving Salonica. You could see most of the Germans loaded with their personal belongings on their back walking towards bus terminals or train depots or just walking with their heads down as if they knew their resting period in Greece was over and hard days were coming for them soon, most likely on the Russian front.

One warm day of the late summer while keeping away from the factory, I felt warm and entered a bar to get a refreshing beer. While I was seated on a high stool, I turned my face to see who was coming to sit next to me and I noticed two Germans, loaded with all their belongings on their backs, and to my unexpected surprise, I stared and recognized the German next to me to be "Hans," the well-known and hated German who was stationed for a few years in my hometown Archanes and by whom I had gotten a beating a couple of times.

Hans was known to all as a forceful but comical guy. He must have been in my hometown for two years, and a year and a half after that incident, I happened to meet him in Salonica ready to be shipped out, obviously going to Russia where the situation would be grave. With great probability, he would be doing forced labor for the Russians, months afterwards. Whatever goes around, comes around they say.

As soon as I recognized him, I turned the other way and left. I didn't think he recognized me, but even if he did, he was no longer a threat; I had explained my way out of more serious and dangerous situations since our last encounter, and I had no interest explaining to him what I was doing in Salonica.

In a couple of weeks after that, we realized that most of the Germans had left. You could hardly see any Germans walking in the streets, so after meeting with Yiapitzoglou and the others, we decided to go back and start communication with Cairo again. We did not think the Germans would be looking for us anymore, so we went back to the factory and we were glad

Hans was a tall blond German with a strong commanding air, which gained him a job of rounding up temporary labor for various jobs needed to accommodate the Germans stationed in my hometown.

Because he needed help daily, every time Hans was seen coming to our market place, word was quickly passed that, "Hans is coming, Hans is coming." And everybody went running to hide.

One day as I came out from our house, which happened to be next to the market, I saw Hans collecting people for that day's labor, and before I had a chance to hide, he grabbed me. He had three other civilians who had been grabbed previously, so there were four of us; and Hans proceeded toward the center of the market. While we all were walking, Hans saw another man in a cafe house and went to grab him, and as soon as he turned his back, I ran away from him and went for our house to hide. Hans saw me; he let the other four go, just to get me.

While I was running toward our house, I noticed Hans chasing after me. I opened the door and ran inside the house and I went onto the second floor terrace, hoping Hans would leave me alone, but Hans came inside the house chasing after me. My mother saw what was happening and stopped the German telling him aloud, "No *piculo* here, no *piculo* here." (*Piculo* meaning "little boy"). But Hans had a reputation that, "nobody escapes Hans." So he ran up the stairs, hoping that I would not be able to escape from there. Seeing Hans coming up the stairs, I climbed an eight-foot wall; I went onto the roof and put my body in the chimney to hide.

Hans was convinced that it was impossible to have climbed that wall, so he came down the stairs and left. When I knew he was gone, I came down. My mother saw me with my face black from the chimney and she started laughing. In the meantime, she had been worried of Hans's repercussions. Two days later, Hans was collecting people again. He saw me, he grabbed me, and he gave me two strong beatings on my back, using a long stick he was always carrying. He took me, together with three people to a house to help him build an outdoor shower for the Germans to wash themselves. The landlady, on whose yard we were building the shower, was baking bread in an outside oven; and the entire area was smelling so nice to us who were working hard and were hungry. So Hans understood our desires, and without asking the landlady, he went and opened the hot oven, got one big loaf of bread, and he cut it into pieces for us.

to find everything in the covered hole. During the three weeks in which we stayed away, anybody could have gone and taken the wireless, the battery, and the guns. No room had locks, and the factory did not even have doors; the hiding place was at the corner of the factory floor. Next to it was the place where I was operating the wireless. I took every item out from the hiding place and I assembled the wireless again and tried to see if Cairo had given up on me, so at 10:00 AM I sent our signal—"Cando, Cando".

I heard the signal response and I answered. I imagined their happy expression when I answered. First very slow, it became a faster "Cando" indicating to me how glad the operator was to hear from me. Obviously, they thought I had been caught, absent for about a month. I had prepared a small message, explaining why we did not communicate and indicating that we had a close call from being caught and that we had been continuously on the watch for the past thirty days.

Starting communication again, I was kept busy sending one or two telegrams every day of departing ships, trains or group of trucks all going north. It was apparent that the final German evacuation was coming soon. Our people in the harbor notified us that the Germans were placing dynamite along the entire length of Salonica Harbor, including the warehouses that contained millions of pounds of wheat and corn.

"We could not stop them putting dynamite in the harbor but for sure it would be a pity and very unjustified," we said, "if they destroyed so much food since the civilians were starving."

So we notified the archbishop to go and talk to the German high command that was still in Salonica to think of the starving people and change the plans they had to destroy the warehouses.

Unfortunately, the German command did not want to listen to the archbishop either.

The following day the dynamite blew up along the harbor and the warehouses, sinking many ships and throwing hundreds of tons of precious grain in the air for the birds to have a dreamy feast, while thousands in Salonica starved.

I happened to be in that area just before they exploded the dynamite and hundreds of people waited to witness the panoramic view of the explosions. We all cursed the conquerors who, even at the last moment, showed no mercy on the civilians.

That afternoon, we witnessed the last remaining troops to depart, going by foot out from the city in a very long line, carrying their belongings on their backs and the heavy guns loaded on mules or even donkeys.

"Go, go, you animals, Russia is waiting for you," people were saying to them as they saw the conquerors leaving the city with their head lowered from shame. As soon as they left, all the church bells were ringing and everybody was running in the streets dancing and singing patriotic songs. It was a day to remember, a day we were dreaming for three years like the day Greece was liberated from the Turks. Though most of the people looked pale from hunger, the Germans flight gave them back their smile. "We are free, we have been saved," everyone said. For me, it was not only a relief that the Gestapo was not after me anymore, it is a triumph for our organization that no one was caught or killed. It would probably take months," I said, "to feel free and comfortable. But knowing that I survived and that I did a good job made me feel proud of myself, still thanking God that saved me so many times in so many dangerous situations."

Chapter 13

- Arrival of partisans in Salonica, followed by the English troops after the Germans left from the city
- Visit by the American colonel
- Farewell party in a Salonica hotel
- Flight to Athens on a British airplane bomber

After the Germans left, the partisans quicky followed close behind, but since they were inspired with communistic ideas, Cairo suggested that we should not reveal to anyone who we were until the situation settles down; the English and finally the Americans arrived. The partisans were killing anyone who collaborated with the Germans, and we saw many dead people in the streets. So while we were waiting to see what happened. I was sending telegrams of what we observed.

On the way home one day, I saw Sultanitsa, tearing down the walls in the kitchen and washroom. "What are you doing?" I said. She explained to me that the three houses in this complex belonged to a Jewish man who had a thriving lumber business before the war. When the Jews were forced to leave, they could not take their gold with them, so they buried it inside their homes. She was told this by a man who was living in the house. She thought that it could be hidden in the walls of the kitchen or beneath the toilet. She pleaded with me to help her open the wall up to find the gold she thought might be hidden there.

I did not feel right doing this, but just to satisfy her, I took one portion of the wall down. And since I found nothing, I told her that she was misinformed and that we were tearing the walls down for nothing, after all, she would still have to live in that house. She agreed to stop and had someone repair the wall.

A month after the Germans vacated Salonica and the political situation was very unsettled with the partisans, the English came and British troops paraded down the main streets of Salonica and the people were very happy to see them.

While I was waiting to hear my orders, I received a message that an American colonel was coming to Salonica and wanted to know how he would get in touch with me and Yiapitzoglou.

I sent them my address only; I could not give them Yiapitzoglou's address since I did not know it for security reasons. Two days had passed and while I was having breakfast with my landlady, the bell rang and Sultanitsa went to open the door. After she opened the door, she ran inside to me and said, "a car with the American flag on it is outside, would you come out and see what they want?" Immediately, I knew who was coming, and I told my landlady, "They are coming for me!"

"For you? she asked. "Why?"

"I will tell you in a moment," I said. And I went outside. In the American jeep, an American colonel in uniform sat in the backseat, and in the front, there were two American soldiers both in army uniforms.

When I reached the car, the colonel came out from the car; he shook hands with me and he squeezed my both shoulders, saying to me, "I am glad

---

(After I had left Salonica and the partisans came down from the mountains, Sultanitsa sent me a letter, telling me that one day, a partisan came to the house. He said the house was his and went in the kitchen, took a floor panel out next to where Sultanitsa was searching, and pulled out two bags full of English sovereigns. In those bags, she wrote, must had been over two thousand sovereigns. He then opened one bag, telling her, "thanks for keeping this gold safe for me all the time I was out." He was playing with the gold while the hungry eyes of Sultanitsa were staring at them. "The ungrateful owner did not even give me one sovereign," she said. "And now I feel sorry I listened to you, the day you saw me searching for the gold and stopped my search," she wrote. "If I had continued, I would have found it." Poor Sultanitsa!

to know you, Corporal Doundoulakis. I have heard you've done a wonderful job, congratulations. I could have sent the two soldiers to pick you up, but I wanted personally to see the place where you were working.

I would like you to pick up your staff and come with us since the organization has rented a small hotel on the waterfront to stay there till you move out."

"I told him that it would take some time to collect my stuff. After all," I said, "No one knew my real identity."

"Don't worry, Corporal, I understand, take all the time you need. We will wait."

By that time, the traffic had stopped in the street; hundreds of people were asking each other what was going on since it was the first time they ever saw American soldiers. All my neighbors had come out, trying to find out what the Americans wanted from me, the young successful neighbor whom up to that time they thought was a merchant. Across the street, my girlfriend, Annoula, came out with her mother and were asking each other what was happening. Before I went inside to collect my stuff, I thought that it was time to tell my landlady who I was and why the Americans had come there. It was not that easy for me to tell her the truth. All this time she was sheltering an American spy.

"What?" she screamed, "You are an American soldier? You had come from America?"

"Well," I said, "it makes no difference where I came from but I was collecting and sending messages in the factory where you thought we were doing business. Now you see why I did not want you to know where I was going every day."

She started crying when I told her I was leaving and that the American officer was waiting for me. She told her kids that I was leaving, and they all came begging me not to leave. I was like a father to them, the two little girls of three and five years old would sit on my lap everyday; they really had considered me as their father, while I brought them sweets or whatever the kids liked.

After collecting my belongings and before I took them outside, I gave two gold sovereigns to my landlady, and one gold sovereign for each kid and also the grandmother. Then I told Sultanitsa that I would mail her a letter indicating she was sheltering an American soldier for nine months, endangering her entire family, to be given special favor in any American organization, which she thanked me with a last kiss. Then while I was taking my stuff outside, Sultanitsa went to the door and was telling her neighbors very loud for everybody to hear that "Helias is an American soldier, and I knew it all the time." And of course, when everybody heard that, their expression changed to great admiration for me and for her.

Collecting my stuff, I realized I had collected too many things I would not really use; so I told my landlady to keep them. I only took my clothes and, of course, my accordion, which looked like a regular suitcase. I didn't want the colonel to see my accordion in case he thought I was living the sweet life compared to the other underground agents. If he only knew that I was performing concerts every afternoon and that I was the talk of the entire neighborhood!

After loading my stuff in the car and before I jumped in, I turned around and saw all the neighbors, especially the girls across the street, looking at me with sad faces; so I told the colonel if I could have a little more time to say good-bye to them. He, of course, understood perfectly and said, "please take all the time you want, I understand!" All the girls we used to sing together and especially Annoula who had fallen in love with me, were all tearful. They were really very sorry I was leaving. Annoula sadly said, "are you really an American soldier? I will never see you again?"

"Yes," I said, "and as soon as I settle down, I will send you a letter." When she heard that, she smiled a little, and she gave me a good-bye kiss. I shook hands with the girls and neighbors, and at that time, the neighbor I used to talk politics with came, shook hands with me and told me that he had suspected I must have belonged to some type of patriotic organization from what I told him, after the railroad bombardment. "But I would never have suspected you were an American soldier, wow!" he said. "We had an American soldier right under our noses?" We shook hands, and he said, "Don't forget to come and visit us when you are discharged."

"I will do that," I said.

As I was waving good-bye to everybody and was ready to get in the car, I saw another neighbor at his balcony staring at me with a sad face. That man never talked to anyone and all the neighbors thought he was working for the Germans as an informer. That was never verified, but if it was true, he, most likely, said, *How could I have missed him in my neighborhood!*

When I got in the car, I felt sorry I had taken that long to say goodbye; but the colonel was very gracious. He said, "since you were living in this neighborhood for eight to nine months, it was natural to have made a lot of friends and you had an obligation to say good-bye to them." "So don't worry, even if you take longer I wouldn't mind." the colonel said. "After all," he said, "I came to Salonica just for you, there are no other American soldiers here, in fact, it will go down in the record books: an American spy sequestered for almost a year, sending four hundred messages, receiving two hundred and without being caught."

While we started moving, I waved good-bye, and even the colonel was waving goodbye, and we started moving with caution since the street was so crowded with curious people, wanting to find out what an American military car was doing there. A policeman who happened to be there pushed the people back. The colonel then told me he would like to go and see the factory I had used to operate the wireless. It was not far, and in a couple of minutes, we were there. I opened the gate and showed him the yard, the pile of wood we pretended to cut, where the watchman followed the approaching people, etc, and then I took him to the room where I was operating the wireless. I told him that four German officers were staying next door, who almost caught

---

The next time I visited that neighborhood was thirty years later. My wife and I visited Salonica and I took a taxi, telling the taxi driver to take us to Serron 10. When the taxi driver stopped and I looked around, I said to him, "you must be wrong, this is not Serron 10. Instead of one story high homes, as I remembered it, it was six or seven story luxury apartments." The taxi driver asked, "How many years have passed, sir, since you were here?" I said thirty years. The driver then said, "This is Serron 10. Things have changed a lot in the past thirty years." I looked at that luxurious apartment complex and said to myself, *The bags of gold that must have been uncovered by these construction workers!*

me while I was installing the antenna. I showed him the table on which I was placing the wireless, guns, and grenades.

"You mean," the colonel said, "you were sending in this unsecured area? It was open all around you, anybody could walk right in the house, in the factory, in the yard. You must have had guts to operate here, that's all I can say." Then I took him to the place I hid the radio, battery, guns, and grenades. I showed him the pile of lint which hid the plywood cover. I showed him the hole with everything in there.

"My God," the colonel said, "since there are no doors or locks in this place, the police could have come, at anytime and find the wireless, guns, and grenades."
"Well," I said, "we had no other place to hide them, so we thought nobody would suspect there is anything under this pile of lint."

Then the colonel told me that the owners of the factory must have been Jewish. "Look at the Star of David," the colonel said, "exactly above the hole, there was the six-pointed star drawn with red paint."

I told him then that the Jews must have buried their gold in this hole in the ground. "Maybe the owners had drawn this Star of David to remind them where the gold was hidden." said the Colonel. "Who knows, the truth though is that for nine months, nobody came to find my wireless," I said. "The Star of David was enough to keep us safe from harm." The Colonel said "God looked after you Corporal. By the looks of things, you are blessed."

"In general," the colonel said, "I think you were very lucky not to have been discovered." I found out that the Colonel was Jewish, and he was truly happy that I survived.

I showed him the window I jumped out of when I thought the Germans were raiding the factory and he gasped.

I showed him where I was sitting when the German worker opened the door and almost saw me operating the wireless. The Colonel stood there silent. I then told him of the Gestapo lieutenant who warned us not to operate on one Thursday. He refused to believe me on that; he thought I was kidding.

I told him it was true, I really had been warned by the Gestapo and they were just about ready to catch me and they would have caught me if I had not been told to stay away. I told him they had surrounded the block, ready to raid, waiting for me to send a message, I told him we stayed for a month away from this area since the trucks were circling the block every day for weeks, waiting for me to send another message.

"I still say it was a miracle you had not been caught working under these circumstances," the colonel said. He then directed the two American soldiers who were Greek Americans, to take the wireless, guns, and grenades out from the hiding place and took them with us to the hotel where we were going. When we were leaving, Mrs. Eleni, who was occupying the two room apartment, saw us and asked me if the Americans were buying my business, and I said to her, "Yes, Mrs. Eleni, something like that."

"You are doing the right thing, my boy. I always had the impression your business was not doing that well!" I told her good-bye and also whispered in her ear that it would please me if she went and had anything she wanted for free—olive oil, petroleum, charcoal, or firewood before I turn everything over to the Americans.

"Well," she said, "I will think about it!"

I felt I owed a lot to her, the poor old lady who never realized she was living in a hornet's nest.

The colonel heard Mrs. Eleni talking about my business, and I explained to him that we pretended to have business selling olive oil, petroleum, charcoal, and firewood, as our front. He said, "That was a very smart idea. That is another reason why nobody had suspected you."

"Because of the business," I said, "and the help of The Star of David, nobody had suspected us of doing what we were doing, thank God!"

"Yes," he said, "everything helped; but most of all, either you played your role well, or you were just lucky! Don't forget that up to today, five students of the fifteen-people group you attended in Cairo," the colonel said, "were caught and got killed and maybe more, since I have not yet finished my tour of the remaining posts in Macedonia."

"As far as Yiapitzoglou," the colonel said, "I would like to meet him, receive a full detailed report of his service and achievements. Since he is not an American, but a Greek Navy officer, he should report where he belongs. I am only responsible for you," the colonel said. "And we will meet tomorrow to prepare you to go to Athens."

The following day, I met with Yiapitzoglou in the hotel, the OSS had rented for its members, on the waterfront. He told me that before I left for Athens, we should have a party to celebrate our survival and achievements.

So he organized a big party at a big hotel, inviting almost everybody who helped us out. He also had a Greek orchestra playing Greek music till 2:00 AM. We all got drunk and had a wonderful time. Everybody wanted to meet the American phantom, as I was called, since they never knew my name or face.

I found myself the next morning sleeping on a bed in Oreopoulos's house, but I still don't remember how I got there; maybe I was carried there while I was drunk. When I was awakened by Oreopoulos's sister, besides having had a tremendous headache, I still felt wonderful to have known and met so many wonderful families and people.

The following day, the colonel told me, that he was going north to a few cities where other wireless networks had been established; and he invited me to go with him and we would be back in Salonica in two weeks. Then he said, "I will take you to Athens." I told the colonel that if he didn't mind, I would rather go directly to Athens. He said "OK, I will arrange a flight for you."

"By the way," I said to the colonel, "are you going to the city Edessa where the Greek captain Spyros went? I said, "We had come from Alexandria together and had so many unforgettable scary moments, including a German search when Spyros wet his pants from fear?"

"Yes," the colonel said, "that is my first stop," and laughed.

"When you see him, give him regards from Helias, and remind him what I had once told him, that he had nothing to be afraid of, since whatever we were doing, it was only a game!"

"I don't know what you mean, Helias," the colonel said, "but I will give him that message."

The next day, the colonel told me he had found a flight to go to Athens and that I should report to the British office with all my belongings by 10:00 AM in two days, at the Salonica airport. "Our jeep will take you there," he said. I called Yiapitzoglou and told him that I was leaving in two days and I would like to meet with him and Oreopoulos to say good-bye. He told me he was coming right away, and within an hour, he was at the hotel with a bag. "Do you know what is in the bag?" Yiapitzoglou said. "You forgot you had me keep your English sovereigns," he said, "from the 150 of them that were originally in your nylon belt, buying the accordion for twenty-five pieces, and by giving you about five to seven sovereigns a month, you had spent seventy-five, so in this bag there are another seventy-five gold sovereigns. Do you know you can buy an abandoned house right now with these sovereigns? What are you going to do with them? Maybe you should leave them with me, and when you get discharged from the army and we meet again, I will give them to you. Carrying so much gold with you is dangerous, or maybe someone will steal them from you!"

"I know," I said, "they would be safer if I left them with you, but I may need them before the war with Japan is over."

"OK," he said, "be careful with them; they will be useful to you someday." At that time, he met with the American colonel, and after he had given him a full report, hundreds of pages of the organization's nine month's of activities, he told the colonel that I had been acting very bravely endangering myself in order to do my duty, and that I had done a wonderful job and my devoted service was another reason that the organization performed so successfully. Also, he told him that if it was not for Helias' skillful knowledge of German, and his smart handling of dangerous situations, the entire group might have been caught or killed.

We embraced each other and each of us could not help but shed a small tear when we said good-bye. We had passed these dangerous and precarious moments together and now, going in two different directions, we felt like two brothers going apart. We promised that our friendship would not end and we would meet again after the war.

It is to be noted, years passed, but we never stopped communicating, and in year to come, we both had families with children. Our children became good friends and are close to this day.

Chapter 14

Ready for the trip to Athens, as the colonel had instructed me, I was at the British Military office at the airport at 10:00 AM, and I was searching for my transport plane, on which I was going to go to Athens. To my disappointment, they directed me to a British bomber and they told me to load my things. "But where," I said, "there is no room on top. The pilots are sitting up there!"

"You go in the gun turret bubble seat," they told me. It was located under the plane, a small compartment with rounded glass or cupola, in which there was a Browning machine gun for the gunner to shoot at enemy planes during bombing missions. In other words, I could only see downward during flight. But since it could only fit me, with difficulty, where would I put my suitcase in which I had all my clothes and the seventy-five gold sovereigns and of course another case with my accordion. I thought of Yiapitzoglou who pleaded with me not to buy the accordion!

When the pilot saw me with the two suitcases, he told me that they would not fit in the bubble; so he took them and put them in the cargo hold. When I got inside the bubble, I thought I was sitting upside down. When the plane took off, I was afraid to move from the seat, thinking that if I stepped on the glass bubble it might break and I would fall out. It was nice to see the Greek islands and the ocean under your feet, but it was extremely scary especially when the airplane was landing, because before we touched down, I thought we were going to crash on the runway only about two feet off the tarmac!

After that scary flight, I finally arrived safely in Athens, and to my surprise, a jeep was waiting there to pick me up and someone called me with my real name, "Doundoulakis." Up to now, I had been using the name Helias Nicolaou.

In about half an hour's driving, we reached our destination, a five story building with the address Phidias 3 in the central part of Athens. The building was rented to OSS, and I was given a bed on the third floor. The building had big rooms, and might have been an office building previously, with six beds in each big room. I was given a corner bed, and I was told to put my two suitcases under the bed.

Almost everyone in that building wore civilian clothes though we were American soldiers.

Since most had a heavy Greek American accent, I had guessed they belonged to the SO or Special Operations section of OSS. They learned that I was from the SI or Secret Intelligence section and they asked me how long I was in a German-occupied city. When I told them I was there for nine months, they could not believe that I was not caught.

Anyway, everyone obviously had their own hell in the past, and I could see them all just looking around, and thinking of their own dangerous moments and narrow escapes.

The building had no restaurant facilities, so we were given money to eat out. I told myself that while I was walking out in the stores, I should buy a new suitcase since the one I had, had a broken lock. To store seventy-five gold sovereigns, I used some dirty socks. Instead of washing my dirty socks, I bought new pairs and so happened to have about twenty pairs of dirty socks in which I had put all the gold sovereigns. The suitcase had those twenty pairs of rolled dirty socks. Everything else I had collected in the nine months period I was in Salonica, I had left with Sultanitsa. Before I was ready to go out to eat, I tied the suitcase with a thick rope, since I could not lock it, and went out to eat and buy a suitcase. The time was chaotic, the middle of December 1944, just a few days before the civil war had started with the British and the leftist partisans in Athens. Thousands of people were in the streets, either partisans with leftist ideals or right wingers, screaming at each other.

One said, "The Greek king is coming back." The other Greek would say, "The king is dead, and the Russians are coming to save Greece."

In the middle of this upheaval, I had forgotten to buy a suitcase, and when I thought about it, it was too late. "That's all right," I said. "I will buy the suitcase tomorrow." And I went back to the building. As I entered the building, I met with a lieutenant, who was an instructor in the Cairo training school. He told me he was going to meet my brother George in another city of Greece called Volos. Afterwards he would come back to Athens again. He asked me if I wanted to go with him, to act as an interpreter during his trip.

"You are going to my brother?" I said. "Is that where he is? Is he in Volos?" The colonel had told me in Salonica that my brother had done a wonderful job by organizing many thousands of partisans up in the mountains, but he did not tell me where he was. Now that I heard that he was in Volos, only two hours away, I agreed immediately to go with the lieutenant to see my brother.

We agreed that I would meet with the lieutenant at 8:00 AM the following day downstairs. "Don't take much stuff with you," he told me, "since we will be back in Athens in two days." When I went back to my room, I realized I had not bought the suitcase. *Suppose somebody opened the suitcase with the broken lock and stole the seventy-five gold sovereigns?* All night, I was thinking of those gold pieces in an unlocked suitcase under my bed where five other soldiers slept.

Next morning, I decided to take with me twenty gold pieces in case they opened my suitcase and they stole everything. "At least," I said, "I would have twenty of them." I found more rope and I tied the suitcase some more, I wrote my name, rank, and serial number on two sheets of paper and stuck them, with glue on the outside of both the accordion case and the suitcase, and pushed both under my bed.

I met the lieutenant downstairs and left, still thinking of my fifty-five sovereigns being in an unlocked suitcase under my bed, but I felt a little more secure.

We arrived in Volos in about two hours and the lieutenant then said to me, "go now and surprise your brother. He does not know you are coming." I had not seen my brother for about ten months and I remembered the day we said good-bye and good luck to each other. He did not know where I was going and I did not know where he was going.

We both had been trained to be spies and both knew we were going on dangerous missions and maybe that moment could have been the last time we would see each other again. He had told me then that he felt sorry for me, that he got me involved in the resistance movement on Crete, and that this weighed heavily on him. "Now that you are a trained spy," my brother said, "you are not my little brother anymore. I hear you are on the top of the list, and I hope they don't send you to the most dangerous places. Be careful, don't take any unnecessary chances, and good luck on your mission. I am leaving soon," he said, "so let us hope that we both come back alive!" Those good-bye moments with my brother stayed in my mind vividly, and I could not wait to embrace him again.

I asked someone if they knew George Doundoulakis, my brother; and with a smile on his face, he said, "Oh, that is what his name is, Doundoulakis? He was using the name Papadakis." For a moment, I felt sorry I had revealed his real name, but after all, the war was over, and he did not have to hide his real name anymore. I saw him coming down the corridor, and our eyes met; he smiled like the smile that only love brings once in a lifetime. We both were alive, and we embraced. We could not believe we were both finally together again!

He then told me he had organized over 6,500 partisans up in the mountains who were fighting among themselves for political reasons before he went up there to organize them. He was supplying them with American help, bringing many shiploads of food, boots, blankets, and ammunition from Turkey and he was using them for sabotages, in the nearby airports, or German concentration areas or demolition of ships in Volos harbor. He was well-known in that area as the American in charge, and at the liberation parade in Volos he represented the USA, and layed the wreath at the monument of the Unknown soldier.

For his extraordinary work, organizing the partisans in the mountains of Pilion Oros, he was awarded the Legion of Merit. At the time George received the Legion of Merit, seven other medals of Legion of Merit had been given, all to generals, and the exception was George, given to a sergeant. Though he had started as a staff sergeant, he was now a first sergeant. He had jumped from no rank at all to first sergeant in a period of a year and a half.

The following day, the lieutenant I had come with from Athens, received a telegram not to return to Athens since the civil war had started and would be unwise to return.

While we anxiously followed the civil war by radio, we received another telegram not to return to Athens but go to Italy with an English ship that was leaving from Volos Harbor, loaded with Italian prisoners, to Italy. When the lieutenant told me that I had to go with him to Italy and I could not go back to Athens, I could not believe that I would never see those fifty-five gold sovereigns and the accordion.

I said good-bye to my brother again and I went to the English ship, the lieutenant in uniform and me in civies. When we reached the ship, we could not believe our eyes. The top deck of the ship must have had over fifteen hundred Italian prisoners, and most of them were standing and shivering in the cool December we were in. Many had no shoes but rags tied around their feet. All of them were unshaven, dirty and many looked sick.

Our accomodations were much better: they gave us a clean room in which there were two separate beds.

The lieutenant went to eat in the officers' quarters and I went to eat with the soldiers. I noticed, though, that because I had civilian clothes, they refused to give me food, thinking that I was Greek, and since the Greeks were fighting the English, they were mad at all the Greeks. That English behavior made me mad, so I went and spoke to the lieutenant who went to our room and brought me an American army jacket with the American flag on it. I put it on and went back to the same dining room I was in before. The sergeant in that dining room saw me, and though there was a long line of soldiers to be served, he told everybody to let their guest, the American, go ahead and be served, and so I did.

The following morning, I awoke early, hearing a lot of noise and singing. Not knowing what was happening, I put my jacket on and went upstairs. What I saw was unbelievable and difficult to describe; we were entering the harbor of Bari, Italy. And as I found out, the ship was carrying the first Italian prisoners back to Italy, while other ships with thousands of Italian prisoners returning to Italy were sunk by the Germans for revenge, and this ship was bringing the first surviving prisoners.

Since all of Italy had been notified for the arrival of the first ship with prisoners, the wives, parents, and relatives of missing soldiers came, hoping to see if this ship was bringing their loved ones.

As the ship maneuvered slowly inside the harbor, tens of thousands of civilians on the dockside and all the prisoners were singing the Italian national anthem. The prisoners were crying and were ready to swim to shore.

At this time, an English officer saw me up there. He came and told me to go to my cabin, because he said that as soon as the ship docked the prisoners might knock you down in their frenzy and crush you. To my surprise, though, when the ship docked, the lieutenant and I were the first ones called to go out; so I did not witness any happy reunions.

Since the lieutenant was given the address of where to go, with a taxi, we reached our destination. It looked like a hotel, or exclusive resort. The lieutenant turned to me and said, "Being an OSS member has its advantages." After registering, I was sent to a supply room where I was told to get any clothes I wanted, including two uniforms, free cartons of cigarettes, boxes of candy, or chocolates. I was assigned a bed in a beautiful room, which had a wrap around balcony. I went out in the balcony, which was on the second floor and saw to my surprise many people and kids with their hands raised up asking for me to throw them something. It looked to me that Italy, was in a worse condition than Greece and I did not hesitate to go inside and bring the boxes of cigarettes, chocolates, and candies, and I started tossing them to the crowd below. In no time, there were over a hundred people under my balcony. The soldiers at the adjoining room also came out and they joined me throwing stuff, the men asking for cigarettes and the kids for candies. Even a policeman was begging me to throw him something.

When I was registering in the office, the sergeant told me that if I wanted to exchange dollars or sovereigns to Italian liras, I should do the exchange in that office; it was forbidden to do the exchange out in the street. I said OK, but I did not understand the reason. Later on, another soldier told me not to be stupid and do the exchange in the office: outside on the black market I could get three to five times what they give. I understood then that since Italy been liberated only recently, the Italian lira was much devalued and everybody wanted American dollars or gold sovereigns; so on the black market you could get many times more than the official rate of exchange. I was also told in the office that if I was going to be transferred to another country, they would convert the liras into dollars again with the official exchange rate. With twenty-five gold sovereigns in my pockets, I went out in the street wearing my American uniform. I had not even gone a hundred feet, when a well-dressed man approached me and asked me if I had dollars or sovereigns to exchange offering me four or five times the rate of exchange. Without even thinking of the sergeant's warning, I said, "Yes, I have gold sovereigns."

"Follow me, please," he said.

For ten minutes, I was following him through main streets, small streets, and suddenly, we went into a dark alley in which time I got the feeling I made a mistake. He said, "Please, don't be afraid, nothing is going to happen to you." "Right now, you are protected by the Mafia," he said. "Please come in" and he told me to enter a small house. (Years had passed after that incident and still I can't believe I had the courage to follow him). Upon entering a woman came and welcomed me and told me to proceed and follow her. When she told me to go downstairs in the basement, I refused and I wanted to leave. The man then told me that they were working for the Mafia. "And since the Mafia was making money through those money exchanges with the Americans, if anything happened to any American, the Mafia would kill my entire family. Since they had seen me coming here with you, you are safer here than in your place of residence." When I heard that and saw the woman bringing me a glass of orange juice, I calmed down and I trusted them.

He told me to sit down and put on the table what currency I wanted to exchange. Since the rate of exchange was so high, I thought I would have difficulty exchanging them into dollars. Without thinking I said, "I have fifteen gold sovereigns." So I took out fifteen from the twenty-five I had with me. They said OK, and the man calculated on a piece of paper how many liras he would give me. When he came out and he placed on the table a foot and a half high pile of big denominations of Italian liras, I said to myself, *What am I going to do with so much money? Where would I hide them? This time*, I thought, *I will buy a suitcase with a lock.*

The man asked me if I wanted to count them but I wanted to leave, so I said, "I trusted him."

Then the woman brought a cloth bag and put all that money in it and told me that someone outside with a gun would take me to the place I was staying. "We are responsible of your safety," they said, "till you reach your place."

That night, since I had not bought a suitcase yet, I kept all that money inside my bed coverings, next to my pillows, afraid all the money might be stolen. With the rate of exchange at the office, converting liras to dollars, I had calculated I should get a few thousand dollars.

The following day, the captain called me and told me that he had heard about my excellent service in the SI section, and he was very impressed at my accomplishments and that OSS had recommended and honored me with the medal of "Good Conduct and Excellent Performance." He told me that in that afternoon in front of other officers I would be presented with that medal and that I should not forget to be at his office at 3:00 PM.

At 3:00 PM, I was at the captain's office and in front of three other officers, the captain awarded me the medal for which I felt very proud.

Christmas time, 1944, and I remember that it was celebrated with all the particulars, Christmas trees, turkey dinners, and music with Italian bands and singers. Two opera houses, idle during the war, now had performances almost every day so I enjoyed going as many times as I could.

It was not only me who had a lot of money to spend, but every American, who were exchanging their dollars on the black market and they all had plenty to spend. Also, I had realized that since the Americans had brought supplies to Italy, the supply sergeants were selling various items to civilians and their pockets were full of money. I observed that almost every night, big dice games were taking place in the building's basement. The game was getting so wild that you could hear the supply sergeants bid: "shoot $200" or "shoot $300" at the dice games. One time, I saw $5,000 in their hands; other times you would see them with almost nothing.

I had stayed close to two months in that palatial OSS post, and one day, the captain called me and told me that he was sending me back to Cairo to go back to report to the academy I had graduated from. They will tell you where you will go next. I was pleased to hear that I would go back to the palace and meet my classmates, whoever was lucky enough and had survived their mission.

As I was walking away from captain's office, I thought of the million Italian liras I had in my room which had to be exchanged into dollars at the office. So without even thinking of the consequences, I took that pile of liras and placed them on the top of the table of the sergeant's desk. The sergeant checked my record book and saw that I had not exchanged any dollars for liras at all in his office, so he went inside and called the captain. The captain asked me, of course, where I got all that money, so it was apparent that I had gone outside to the Mafia for the exchange, which was forbidden.

He told me, I did something I was not suppose to do, and for that, I would have to be penalized for it. "You were warned not to convert currency with the Mafia, didn't you know that?" the captain said.

Instantly, I told myself that, "I was trained to fabricate stories. I had not forgotten I was taught to lie and I had to find an answer right away! After all, when my life depended on, I had found the proper answer and even the Germans had believed it. "Why not find an answer now?" I said to myself. And instantly I replied to the captain.

"Sir," I said, "have you ever gone down into the basement at night, where the big dice games are taking place almost every evening? Obviously, you have not. That is where I won all those liras. Go tonight, and see what I am talking about. I played a few times, and surprisingly enough, I was very lucky!"

The captain, of course, was not so stupid to believe my story, but since he knew I was an SI agent of the OSS, and had been trained to lie, he looked at me, smiled, and with a softer voice said, "You must be a very lucky man, Corporal. Sergeant, give the corporal the dollars for his liras. Besides, Corporal, it was only last week that I decorated you!" So the sergeant converted all the liras into dollars!

I received a few thousands dollars and I was ready to walk out with them. "You know, Corporal Doundoulakis, it would be smarter to deposit them in the Army bank, and withdraw them anytime, or when you get discharged. After all, you are owed your salary while you were in Greece at $155 per month, and then this money, plus interest, would be a substantial amount when you get discharged. What do you think?"

I agreed with the sergeant, and as I was leaving the office, I said to myself that, "I never expected that whatever I had been taught by the OSS, to be a liar, would ever be so rewarding!"

Next day, I was notified that I had to go to the captain to get my air passage to Cairo. I went to his office, though, did not feel like seeing him again, but I had no other alternative. He told me that he had a hard time finding a ticket from Bari, Italy to Cairo, Egypt for me. Instead, the plane would leave from Naples, so I would have to be driven from Bari to Naples the following morning. I was told to be at 7:00 AM outside the building and a driver would take me to Naples. I woke up at 6:00 AM and I met with the driver, who was driving a truck. The truck had side bar seats, each side inside the truck. Though the truck was covered only with a canvas on its top and back, it was very cold inside. The roads had more than a foot of snow that freezing day of winter in February 1945; it was so cold that I was freezing just sitting in that truck. There were another five soldiers in the same truck; they called the driver and complained about the lousy means of transportation provided, but the driver told us to bear with it since the entire trip would take less than an hour. In reality, we were three hours on those snow covered roads, and when the truck had to go uphill, the tires were spinning and the truck did not move. The driver said he had forgotten to get chains for the wheels, so he had decided to go back. It took us another two hours to come back and he told me to go back to the captain and get air tickets for tomorrow's flight, reminding me not to forget to be out at 7:00 AM, tomorrow, ready to go. As soon as we arrived, I ran to the captain and, as soon as he saw me, he said, "what happened? The plane refused to accept you?" I told him about the delay with the truck. He gave me new air tickets and told me they were the last available, so not to miss the flight.

I went to my room; I set my alarm for 6:00 AM, but, did not turn it on, and when I woke up the following morning it was 8:00 AM. "My God," I said, "I did not wake up, what am I going to do? I am not going to that captain again, he will throw me out and this time, I agree, he would be right for it." "That truck driver," I said, "why didn't he come and wake me up?" For an hour, I was thinking what to do; as a matter of fact, I said to myself, "I would be willing to give all my saved money if I could find a public air transportation to take me to Cairo."

After thinking for an hour, I decided to go to the captain again and I did. As soon as he saw me, he smiled a little bit and then he said, "I cannot get rid of you, Corporal, can I?" I just don't want to hear your excuse again, I know you always have or fabricate one but this time you are lucky, I just got two tickets, which were returned to me, so I guess, you can have one." I could not find words to thank him for not throwing me out, but I kept quiet, took the ticket, and left. The following night, I had two alarm clocks plus I went and told the driver that I would give him $20 to come and wake me up at 7:00 am, in case I did not wake up. Since I froze the first time, I put on long johns, jackets, double sweaters, plus an overcoat and I did not feel cold. We arrived in Naples and, of course, I entered the airplane with layers of clothing on. When we reached Cairo, a few hours from then, the temperature was over ninety degrees Fahrenheit, and I had difficulty in breathing. They told me that I should go outside and find a car that was waiting to pick me up and take me where I was supposed to go. I found the car and the driver and soon as he saw me said, "Gosh, where did you come from, Alaska?"

It was easy to take off the overcoat, the double sweaters, the jacket, but not the long johns and double socks!

We were four soldiers, and three of them had orders to go outside Cairo. The driver saw where I had to go, and he told me that I was different "you must be of higher rank, yes?" "No," I said, "just a different job."

"I understand," the driver said. "Maybe I shouldn't ask too many questions!"

Then he asked me if I did not mind taking the other three soldiers to their place first, even though it was a little further than my place. He said that he did not want them to see where some other soldiers live and get, of course, disappointed.

I agreed, and said to him "yes, go ahead. After all, if they saw me go into that place, what would they think?"

Chapter 15

- Return to the palace school in Cairo, Egypt
- Unexpected recovery of the lost accordion and fifty-five gold sovereigns

I couldn't wait to reach the palace school, and when the driver brought me and left me outside of the palace, he turned to me and said, "I wonder what qualification you got to have in order to stay in a place like this!" I answered him with only one word: "Guts!"

It was so wonderful to come back to the palace school, so when we reached the main gate, I opened and walked right into the main hall. Most of my instructors were there, knew I was coming and they all were so glad that I was back. It was that time when I heard about the five students from the fifteen who were caught and killed. Two of the five were the Yugoslavians with whom I was playing ping-pong together almost every day. All the instructors wanted to know where I went and if I had a rough time and if the Gestapo ever came close to catching me and, most important if my training had helped me in performing my job. They were very glad when I told them that without their instructions I would have been caught, even on the first day.

When I went to my room, I found my old uniform, which I put on. But now I inserted my medals, ribbons together with a star, indicating that I had taken part in front line action. I looked in the mirror and said to myself, I was never caught, I was never tortured, I was back alive.

The next day, I wanted to go to Cairo and meet with my relatives. On a school bus, I went to Cairo, and when they saw me, they were anxious to hear what had happened to me in all that time. They had not heard from me for over ten months. I told them where I had gone and they listened with awe. A young cousin of mine named Nicos kept on asking me to recall the dangerous episodes when I was almost caught by the Gestapo.

"To celebrate my return," I told them, "I would like to take you all to a night club, the best one in Cairo, called Bridge de Pyramid." To my surprise, fifteen of my relatives wanted to come, and since I had to pay for their admission and drinks, it cost me four or five monthly salaries.

Around March 1945, my brother George came back from his mission to Pilion Oros. I did not forget to mention to him that as a result of my visit to him in December, I had left fifty-five gold sovereigns in an unlocked suitcase under my bed, and since I was not able to come back to Athens, I had lost them together with my accordion. He felt sorry for me losing those precious things, but he said not to worry, at least I had come back alive.

I felt very proud for my brother who also, had received from England the "King's Medal of Courage," England's highest decoration given to civilians, for his role as leader of a resistance group on Crete, during 1941 to 1943.

In the beginning of April 1945, we were told that my brother and I would be sent to United States, and we started collecting our belongings when the supply sergeant came to me and asked me how I spelled my name and if my first name was Helias. I said, "Yes, my name is Helias."

"Well," he said, "a few days ago, two suitcases had come through the army delivery service from Italy. And he could not read the last name, since it was torn out, and he wanted me to see if these suitcases belonged to you." "What?" I said, "Two suitcases, you got two suitcases?"

After my brother had come back, he was notified to go to OSS headquarters in Cairo to receive the Legion of Merit. It also said that he is to bring his brother with him since the office knew that I was also staying in the same school.

We both went to the OSS headquarters and I witnessed a two-star general deccorating and was congratulated by ten high OSS officials who had been invited for the ceremony also. Besides the Legion of Merit, the general gave him another medal the "Good conduct and excellent performance" medal.

"Yes," he said, "please come and see if they belong to you. I don't know what to do with them."

I ran with him, and I could not believe my eyes; in front of me were my two suitcases!

The accordion and the other suitcase, still tied still unlocked. Only the first name was readable and the last name only the first four letters Doun . . . but my serial number was still there, 10675040, reading the papers, stuck on them, it showed that they went from Athens, to Bari, Italy, and from Bari, Italy, they were sent to Cairo OSS headquarters, and then to the school where I was staying, traveling for a period of three months. I could not wait, I had to take them to my room and open them to find out if my fifty-five gold sovereigns were still in there. I took them to my room, I cut the ropes, and I took out the shirts, which were on the top. And under the shirts, I could see the twenty dirty socks with the fifty-five gold sovereigns in them.

Rewarded for Courage, Patriotism

George receiving the Legion of Merit by
General Giles at OSS HQ in Cairo, 1945

"Gosh," I said, "an unlocked suitcase went around the Mediterranean, carrying a treasure in it, and nobody found it?"

When I told my brother that I had found the fifty-five gold pieces, he suggested that I still keep them in that unlocked suitcase if I didn't want them to be stolen.

Since I did not dare play my accordion on the school premises and be forced to tell them why I had bought it, I took it to my relatives' house and played a few Greek song to them. They had enjoyed my playing so much that I decided to leave it there and play it for them till I was ready to leave for United States.

Next time I visited them, my cousin Popi started crying when I told her to give me my accordion to play. Popi was married to a man who liked to drink, and he was drunk most of the time when he was home. Obviously, he wanted money to buy alcohol, so he took the accordion secretly and sold it. My cousin felt very embarrassed when she found out what her husband had done, they had a big fight. She wanted to find money to pay me, but of course, she did not know that it had cost me twenty-two gold sovereigns. Anyway, that was the end of my accordion, lost again, but this time, I knew, it would not miraculously re-appear!

Since we had nothing to do before we got the final OK to leave for United States, and with plenty of time to relax, I thought of the yacht only a walking distance from the school on the river Nile. I said to myself that most likely, I would never have another chance to enjoy a 150 foot yacht, so why not take advantage and visit it.

I thought that by showing my OSS identification card, I could walk around the deck or inside the boat, which had a restaurant, an entertainment room, and even an exercise room." I felt that soon enough, I will leave, and the 150 foot yacht and all those special luxuries, so, now that I could still enjoy them, why not take advantage on them. Every time I had visited the yacht, I was asked if I wanted a ride and refused. But now that I was to leave for United States, I said, "why not, would I have another chance to go sailing on the Nile?"

The following morning I asked my brother if he wanted to visit the yacht and go for a sailboat ride and of course, he said, "No!". And then, he added, I thought the spying around should have made you a grown man, but I see you are still a kid."

"George," I said, "the difference between you and me is that you think I am still a kid because you were born thinking as an adult and you are missing the joys of life. Sailing is done by adults who know how to live, not by people like you whose only pleasure is reading a science book." I got mad, and left.

Since the boat was only a short walking distance I left, showed my OSS I.D. and entered the yacht. As I was walking on the top deck I saw the Arab in charge who asked me again if I liked to go for a ride. This time, he was very happy to hear my "yes" reply and told me to follow him. The sailboat, which was over forty feet long was tied next to the big yacht and after we got in and he opened the sails I felt the boat was not that stable at all. Though the sailboat was not that small it was still leaning one way or the other with the wind, and obviously, I was looking scared, so the man said not to worry since that is the joy of sailing. I enjoyed it for about an hour but when the wind picked up I told him to go back; I did not want to fall out in that fast moving river current. I was satisfied though the ride was short, that I finally sailed the Nile

In April of 1945, my brother and I were told that we were leaving for United States.

After getting our voyage in order, we saw that our destination was Miami Florida. Since we had no home address in United States, we did not say anything. Our parents were on Crete; we had nobody in the USA since we had left America for Crete when I was two. And we were coming back after so long, so it did not make any difference where they were sending us; we said good-bye to all the instructors, including the director of the school, now Colonel Vassos, who shook our hands and said he was proud of both of us. We both had proved to the OSS organization how excellent the training had been. "Not only did you do a wonderful job but you both came back alive; not only did we teach you how to do your job right, but we taught you how to avoid being caught." And he said, "I am more glad on your second achievement." Then the Colonel turned to another officer and pointing to me, said," The German Gestapo gave up on him, he was too well trained to be caught." We shook hands, I saluted him, and said goodbye.

After we had breakfast a jeep was going to take us to the airport, and as we were leaving, we had a last look at that magnificent building with the many colored marble apartments and the beautiful gardens and its memories.

We arrived at the airport on time, and we got into the airplane, and after a couple of hours, we arrived in Casablanca where we slept that night. The following morning, after breakfast we left and went to the Canary Islands where everyone ate breakfast again. Breakfast again, don't they like lunches? Then I realized we were traveling westward, catching up to breakfast-time wherever we went. We finally arrived in Miami, for lunch.

DECORATION BY THE GREEK GOVERNMENT

World War II Medals received.

The two brothers after completion of their successful assignments

Chapter 16

• Arrival in Miami, Florida, April 1945

We arrived in Miami, and if the pilot wanted to give us a sightseeing tour, he couldn't have done it better! We were told we were going to sleep overnight in Miami, and that the following day, would leave for Washington DC, by train. That afternoon, we felt like touring the city, and we boarded a bus to take us to Miami Beach, which, as we were told was the hottest place to visit in Miami. We took a bus, and going over a causeway, we arrived in Miami Beach, which had beautiful hotels near a park that was at the tip of Miami Beach. North of this point, was vacant land. As we were sitting on a bench in the park watching the water, a gentlemen approached us, introduced himself to us, gave us his card, and said that he was a salesman at the real estate office across the street. He said that he was selling land north from Sixtieth Street. He asked us if we had any money to put down as a deposit to buy land he was selling. He showed us a map and he said, "The more you proceed north of Sixtieth Street, the cheaper it is." He persuaded us to follow him to his office and he showed us small or large lots of waterfront property, which we would own, with a small reasonable deposit.

In my pockets were fifty five gold sovereigns and one thousand dollars in cash, and a savings account passbook with three to four thousand dollars. I trusted the man, but my brother George was skeptical, and convinced me that I would surely lose all my money on "alligator infested land." He finally made me change my mind and I told the man we were not interested. Right after Miami Beach started expanding very rapidly, and from the Sixtieth Street, it has now been developed to 250th Street, My fifty-five gold sovereigns would have become millions of dollars.

In New York, my brother told me that he was investing in a cargo ship registered in Greece; so I did the same and gave most of the money I had, which were lost within a short time. When I happen to go to Miami Beach, I remember that man and get mad at myself for not buying that property and not listening to my gut feelings.

Chapter 17

- Arrival in Washington DC and stationed at the Congressional Club, another luxury for returning OSS members
- Requesting transfer out of the Congressional Club

The following day, George and I went to the railroad station and were told that we had been assigned to two births in a Pullman, and after sixteen hours, we finally arrived in Washington DC. After calling OSS HQ, a jeep driven by a soldier, came and picked us up. Going through the streets, we saw barricades all over the main avenues. "Was there a parade?" we asked. The driver said that the funeral procession had just driven by for President Franklin Delano Roosevelt, who was buried this morning. "Harry S. Truman is now our new president," the driver said. "What," I said, "George, how could we have missed it, didn't you hear anyone say anything?"

We left Washington DC, and in about fifteen minutes, we arrived at our destination. "What is this?" "Another resort!"

The driver said that this was the Congressional Club and was used for relaxation by the congressmen and to meet on weekends. "Now its been assigned to OSS personnel only, forget it. I don't know, but I was told to bring you here," the driver said.

We went to the reception desk, and a lady who welcomed us told us where our rooms would be. We asked her if this is the place we would be staying, and she said yes. "The Congressional Club," she said, "is a resting quarters for *chosen* OSS members, returning from important assignments."

We just could not believe it. That club, besides being a wonderful building, had dancing halls, exercise rooms, billiard rooms, and many living quarters. Outside it had an artificial lake with fishing provisions and next to it was a tremendous golf course. Jokingly, I told my brother that we were so tired living in palaces and villas. "Do we have to live in country clubs?"

He laughed and said, "let us continue enjoying this royal treatment while it is offered to us. After we leave the OSS and get discharged, we will only dream of the good times we had."

There was a bus leaving from the club to go to Washington DC, four times a day so that we could go to the city anytime we wanted. Every Friday night, USO girls were keeping us company, and we danced the nights away. We could not have dreamed of a better place to be. For the last two months I was relaxing at the palace in Cairo, visiting my relatives, and friends, and enjoying myself on the OSS yacht, or entertaining myself in the many activities the palace offered. "Now in this country club, maybe I should learn how to play golf or fish!"

Two months or more passed and, unreasonably enough, I had gotten bored doing nothing but enjoying myself. After all, I had been trained to be a "spoiled kid" and I did not know what I wanted. So while I visited some Greek American soldiers in Washington DC, they told me that they were also members of the OSS, in the SO or special operations group. And now they were guards at the OSS HQ in Washington DC, and were living in a nearby hotel at night. They said they had a wonderful time after working hours in the hotel where many girls stayed. They persuaded me to come and be a guard with them and to get accommodations in the hotel, where I'd have the time of my life.

Without thinking, I went to the captain and told him that I was bored that I would rather be a guard like those other Greek Americans at OSS HQ.

He listened, and with a little smile on his face, he called in the sergeant, who was in the adjoining room, and he told me to repeat what I had said to him before the sergeant. "Sergeant," the captain said, "please listen to the corporal. He says he is bored and tired, doing nothing in this country club and he wants to be transferred to Washington."

"If that is what you want, Corporal," the captain said, "you can have it but if you leave from here, you cannot come back."

"I agree," I said to the captain. And he told the sergeant to make the arrangements to report to OSS headquarters as a guard. Also, he was going to give me money to find a hotel.

The following Monday, I reported to guard duty at the office in Washington where I was told that the only thing I would have to do was to stand guard in front of the main entrance of OSS Headquarters and not allow anyone in unless he showed his OSS identification card to me. A lady who was responsible for the guards pointed out to me that if someone was forcing himself in, I should initiate an alarm, a hidden button under the rim of the desk where I was stationed, to initiate help from heavily armed guards inside.

A week passed with no difficulty and I enjoyed the evenings in the hotel where my friends and I were staying. There were plenty of girls just as they said, and I thought I had made the right move.

During the second week, however, while I was at my post in the front entrance, a two-star general arrived by a car at the front entrance, and without showing me an identification, he proceeded right by me. Without observing his rank and without knowing who he was, I stopped him and asked to see his identification. He stopped, of course, he put his hand in his pocket, took his identification out, and very politely showed it to me. He continued on his way. Five minutes had not passed, and the lady in charge of the guards ran down the corridor, screaming bloody murder!

"What did you do! What did you do, you stopped and asked the identification from a two-star general who happens to be the big boss of OSS headquarters?"

I stopped her and told her that, "my instructions were that everyone must show his identification and that I should not allow unidentified personnel through that door unless he shows me his identification."

"Yes," she said, "everyone, but not from him!"

"Suppose he was a spy," I said.

"If someone had the courage,' she said, "to come inside this place pretending to be a general, and is not recognized, then we deserve to be shut down!"

'In your case, you insulted the general, and because of that, you are fired. Go back where you came from!"

With my head down, I went back to the captain at the Congressional Club and told him what had happened. He said that he could not take me back, but he would find some other job to do till I got discharged. "Oh," he said, "I need someone to burn confidential papers in the building you were fired from, so please go to that basement and they will tell you what to do." I went to the basement and someone showed me how to burn papers outside in the yard. Away from the building, they had a round, fenced pit in which I would burn discarded confidential papers. Since there were piles of bags, full of papers to be burned, there was a lot of smoke, which with a little wind, was going in my eyes and I was coughing excessively. I could not bear the job any longer and in three days or so, and with my eyes red from the smoke, I again found myself in front of the captain's desk. "What is the complaint this time?" he asked me.

I told him that the job he had given me had made me sick and that I could not continue any longer. He told me to report back in a couple of days to decide what to do with me. "You should never have left the Congressional Club," he said to me!

The next time I reported to the captain, he told me that he could not find any job for me. But since I had never had basic training, he had thought to send me back to boot camp and train me and let somebody else find out what to do with me until I got discharged. "Why don't they discharge me now," I said.

"Well, when the war is completely over, the ones with most years in service have the priority. You only have two years in service to this day."

Chapter 18

- Basic Training in Camp Crowder, Missorri.

I was finally being sent to the Camp Crowder, Missouri, to initiate my army basic training, and may be to learn to behave like a soldier, since the captain did not know what to do with me in Washington and I had not appreciated what I had been offered. He wanted to send me to a place I thought I did not deserve, a training that would have no purpose, a pure unnecessary punishment, after what I had been through.

The next day, the captain told me he was sending me to Camp Crowder, and since I had no choice, I accepted. After a two day train ride, from Washington, I reached the camp, and as I was told, I reported to the admissions office.

My direct orders from the captain in Washington DC indicated that I should be put into basic training and be occupied until discharge. When I reported to the admitting office, where a colonel was in charge, the colonel looked at me. He saw the good conduct medal, and excellent performance medal on me, and a star on the top of the European ribbon, plus he saw I was a paratrooper, so he asked the sergeant to show him my records, which the sergeant got and gave to him.

After the colonel read the report very carefully, he called me to come to his office. He also called the captain under him and two lieutenants. The colonel turned to the other officers and said, "You are going to witness today a bad assignment by another officer." The corporal here is a member of the OSS since he was enlisted in the American army two years ago. He had five months of spy training, and he performed a nine-month mission in Greece. He was decorated for his excellent performance, and now they send him here to get basic training since he never got it since they don't know what to do with him until he gets discharged. "My God, isn't this the craziest decision by an American officer?" Then he turned to me and said, "Did you really finish that queer spy training course?"

"Yes, sir," I said. "I was taught how to steal, how to lie, and how to cheat. That is why I am getting cheated in the end. Since my brother and I had previous underground experience, OSS begged for us to join them, being American citizens. They needed spies to be sent back to Greece but they could not find qualified people. I was sent into the most dangerous city in Greece, sent four hundred messages while the Gestapo was after me. My valuable messages killed thousands of Germans and I cheated the Gestapo's plans to get me over half a dozen times. On one time while I was transmitting, the Gestapo surrounded the block on three corners and I jumped out from a rear window and escaped in the nick of time."

"And your superior in Washington DC," the colonel said, "knowing your record, sent you here for basic training!"
"Actually," I said, "it was my fault. I would still be enjoying the Congressional Club facilities till I got discharged, but I had not appreciated it, and I am getting punished for that now. It was my stupidity that has brought me here. Even if the captain in charge back in DC were here, it is still up to you to decide if I should be excused from basic training while I am waiting for my discharge papers."

At that point, the colonel told the officers to go back to their duties, and then he turned to me and said that I had gone through enough in the war and that he didn't think I deserved the punishment of basic training. "Why do you need this torture just before you get discharged?"

So instead, he assigned me to an English language class to improve my English till the time of my discharge.

I wanted to improve my English anyway, to be able to attend college later on, so I liked that idea very much.

Camp Crowder was one of the biggest training camps in United States, with over forty thousand people. Its adjoining little town, Joplin, Missouri, had a population of five hundred people but had six movie theatres, besides the four movies that were in the camp, twenty bars, and a few restaurants. It was strictly a GI town. I was obliged to attend the school eight hours a day, five days a week, and after that, I entertained myself in the many playgrounds or going to the movies.

In the spring of 1946, I was notified finally that my turn came to be discharged and that meant that I had to make plans for my future. No more palaces, country clubs or mess halls where they cared for me or gave me food. From now on, I would have to work for it. I had to decide if I should go through many years of hard work in colleges or learn some type of trade and forget college. Up to now, I had considered life to be just a game, which though it included dangerous moments, was very interesting. Would my future life be more interesting? No doubt, I would have to work hard, from now on, to earn a living on my own, and prepared myself for that.

Epilogue

Postwar Achievements

- Discharge from the army, at Fort Dix, New Jersey
- Choosing Brooklyn NY as my hometown
- Attended college
- Received a Masters in Civil Engineering
- Marriage to Rita, my wife for fifty-five years, raised four sons, and have seven grandchildren

After more than six months in Camp Crowder, I was notified that my turn had come to get discharged, and to get discharged, I would have to go to Fort Dix in New Jersey. There I was examined by army doctors, who told me that I must have broken my nose in the fall I took while installing the wireless antenna, I was granted a disability pension, which made me a disabled veteran. Everything was going well with my discharging process until I was asked for my home address. I told them I did not have one, since my parents were still in Greece, and I had left the United States twenty year ago. "You must give us an address," the sergeant said, "in order for you to receive mail." At that moment, I remembered that my father had a cousin living in Brooklyn, so I looked in the telephone book, and fortunately, I found her name and address, so I gave that address to them. At least I knew I was going to Brooklyn to a cousin, who had never heard of me probably.

I said to myself, *If I go to her house and introduce myself, she would help me find an apartment to rent near her area. I had plenty of money in my pockets, an Army bank book and also some gold sovereigns.*

I thought, *Maybe it would be better if I called her first, introduce myself, and tell her that I would be coming to her house, than if I just went without any notification.* So I called her, and to my surprise, she was extremely happy to hear who I was and offered me a place to stay until I got my own apartment. When they asked me where my home was, I said loudly, "Brooklyn, New York." Then the sergeant brought me and gave me a railroad ticket, saying, "Penn Station, New York City." Since I had never been in Brooklyn before and did not know that Brooklyn was part of New York City, said to the sergeant, "Sergeant this ticket says to go to Penn Station, New York City; I want to go to Brooklyn!" The sergeant stared at me, and with a low tone of voice said to the others, "Here is a guy who does not know how to go home. *"My God! We sent people like this overseas, and we still won the war?"*

I heard him, but I did not really understand what he meant so I said nothing! The soldier next to me turned to me and told me not to worry that I had the right ticket.

With my suitcase in one hand and a big army bag on my shoulder, I walked to the railroad station where I found the train that was going to New York. In a short time, the train entered Pennsylvania Station, in New York City. I was anxious to see the skyscrapers in Manhattan and I went upstairs. I admired the Empire State Building next to the station. It was my first look at New York City in twenty years, when my parents and I left from the New York docks, by ships, for Crete. After admiring the buildings for a while, I showed the address to a policeman and I asked him to show me how I could go to Pacific Street, Brooklyn.

He of course, told me that in order to go to Brooklyn I would have to take a subway and he told me, which one to take. Since he understood that I was in New York for the first time and I did not even know what a subway was, volunteered to take me back to Penn Station to the proper subway and told me to follow the map and get off at the proper station.

I enjoyed the ride, and I was thrilled with the speed the trains were going, knowing, we were going under the East river from Manhattan to Brooklyn. I got out from the train at the proper station and walked toward the address, 251 Pacific Street. To my surprise, my aunt's apartment was on the fifth floor and there was no elevator. It was very difficult to carry my suitcase and the army bag up to the fifth floor. That stairway took me a long time to climb, and when I was finally on the fifth floor I was exhausted.

My Aunt Zambia was more than happy to see me and I stayed with her a few days. In the meantime, my brother had also gotten discharged and we both tried to rent a small apartment together but we were unable to find anything except an attic in a very old house. The one we found had a big room with toilet facilities on the third floor in a large private home. Since it was an attic apartment, the temperature was getting close to one hundred degrees Fahrenheit in the summer months, and we made use of a small fan.

It was quite a difference in living conditions between Brooklyn and the Cairo palace or the Congressional Club!

We applied immediately to college and I was told that while I was going to college, I would get 150 dollars a month plus all schooling and books paid for being a disabled veteran, under the GI bill. I realized and now appreciated my brother's persistence, two and a half years ago, at the time of enlistment to join OSS as soldiers and not civilians, as OSS had first proposed. And as a disabled veteran, I had an unlimited time for schooling. Up to that time I had cursed those bridge-playing German officers for my fall, but almost two years later I realized that to everything there is a silver lining.

Taking advantage of the free schooling I struggled for five years in colleges to become a civil engineer, what I always wanted to be. It was very hard to attend the difficult engineering courses with my poor grasp of the English language. Five hard years passed, though, in which time I persevered studied hard, and lived up to the American dream.

I am thankful that I never gave up my schooling. Having been through many dangerous missions and escaped miraculously, I felt honored that the United States of America rewarded me with the opportunity of unlimited educational benefits. I went to college for five years and received an associate, bachelors, and a master's degree in civil engineering.

Also, I studied hard and passed the test to became a "Professional Engineer" in two states, New York and Virginia.

At that time, while earning a good salary, I was very lucky to become acquainted with a very nice family, the "Gianoplus Family", who had a beautiful daughter named Rita, with whom I dated, got engaged, and married in 1952. Having had a very happy life together, married for fifty-five years, we have four sons: James, a prosthodontist, Stephen, a neuroradiologist,

Plato, an environmental engineer, and Thomas, a chemist. We have seven beautiful grandchildren.

Below are described some of my professional accomplishments, and I am proud to say, they are classified as world famous achievements.

I had no difficulty in finding desirable jobs in building design. At the time the sixty-five story, Pan Am (now MetLife) skyscraper, over the Grand Central Station in New York was being designed. I was hired, after the chief engineer saw that I had a master's degree, specializing in large foundations and was assigned to this project and did the leading design for the skyscraper's foundation.

The greatest engineering accomplishment of mine as a civil engineer, however, is that I possess and hold the only patent that exists in the design of the Arecibo Antenna, the largest radiotelescope antenna in the world.

My brother, who also had an extensive education earned a master's in electronics and who happened to be the director of research of an antenna company in New York, called General Bronze Corp. He had received from Cornell University, in 1959, an invitation to design the suspension system for the largest radiotelescope antenna in existence. Consulting with me, we studied the topographic maps where the antenna was planned to be built. We concluded that to suspend the antenna feed assembly, having a weight of eight hundred tons about 450 feet above the one thousand foot diameter stationary reflector, would best be supported with a cable system, and our design was adapted later on and the antenna was so constructed. Cornell University on the other hand, had proposed an enormous tripod-like structure, which would cost twice as much. The world famous radiotelescope at the National Astronomy and Ionosphere Center in Arecibo, Puerto Rico has been declared by TLC (Learning Channel) as the greatest and most fascinating structure in the world. Its suspension system was patented by Helias Doundoulakis (#3,273,156 in Sept. 13, 1966), and I am proud to say, is my crowning achievement.

During the early years of 1962 when the space program prepared to send men to the moon, I inquired about a job at Grumman Aerospace, and with my qualifications, I had no difficulty getting the proper job. Since I had been hired at the beginning of the project, I took part in the actual design of the legs, the oxygen tanks, and various other parts of the LEM (Lunar Module). I worked eleven years in the space program, some of those as a group leader in ground support design, structural integrity and inspection of supporting structures. I shook hands with many astronauts and my signature, signed on a plaque with others, was left by the first two groups of astronauts of Apollo 11 and 12 on their landings on the moon.

After fifty-five years of a happy married life and after forty years of a rewarding engineering career, I find myself retired at the age of eighty-four with old age pains, trying to satisfy my never-ending curiosity. What if the German guard who searched me outside of Salonica never had a son who looked like me, and was not so distracted from his duties that he found my hidden pistol?

I led a full life, everything given with plenty of excitement, enjoyment, and rewards, which I can summarize up in one final sentence:

My life was a game that had many interesting faces, had been played dangerously but generally was played the proper and, luckily enough, the winning way!

The Polytechnic Institute of Brookl

To all unto whom these Presents shall come or may concern

GREETING

Know Ye that We, the Corporation of the Polytechnic Institute of
Virtue of the authority conferred upon us by our Charter from the Reg
University of the State of New York, and upon the recommendation of t
our said Institute, from which it appears that

Helias J. Doundoulakis

has satisfactorily completed our course of study requisite for this Degree
admit him to the Degree of

Master of Civil Engineering

and do confer upon him all the honors and privileges appertaining there

In Witness Whereof We have caused this Diploma to be signed by the
our said Institute, by the Secretary of the Faculty, and by the Chairman and
the Corporation.

The National Aeronautics and Space Administration

presents the

Apollo Achievement Award

to

HELIAS DOUNDOULAKIS

In appreciation of dedicated service to the nation as a member of the team which has advanced the nation's capabilities in aeronautics and space and demonstrated them in many outstanding accomplishments culminating in Apollo 11's successful achievement of man's first landing on the moon, July 20, 1969.

Signed at Washington, D.C.

ADMINISTRATOR, NASA

"The many articles in English and Greek
about the author and his brother."

National Ethnic Coalition of Organizations Foundation, Inc.

January 7, 1999

Mr. Helias J. Doundoulakis
3218 Ann Street
Baldwin, NY 11510

Dear Mr. Doundoulakis:

We are very pleased to advise you that you have been nominated as a candidate to receive the 1999 *Ellis Island Medal of Honor.* This nomination was sent in by John Catsimatidis.

This year's event will be held on Saturday, May 8th. Traditionally, both the Ceremony and the Gala Dinner take place in the historic Great Hall on Ellis Island.

The Medal is presented to outstanding American citizens from all walks of life who have distinguished themselves among their specific ethnic groups. These individuals are recognized for their significant contributions to this country. In 1986, the *Ellis Island Medal of Honor* was sanctioned by Congress and has since been recognized in the *Congressional Record* by an annual listing of the individual recipients.

Your nomination will be included with those that have been received in response to a widely publicized national poll and public service announcements in mass media and the Internet. The nominations will be submitted to one of our forty-three ethnic screening groups who will then make recommendations to our Board of Directors for final selection. **Only citizens of the United States will be considered.**

It may interest you to know that six Presidents of the United States have received this award, as well as many Members of Congress, Noble Prize winners, prominent scientists and such outstanding military heroes as Generals Norman Schwartzkopf and Colin Powell.

It is required that you be present Saturday, May 8th on Ellis Island to receive this award, so please advise us in writing, as soon as possible, as to whether or not you will be available. I have enclosed descriptive material to illustrate the vast scope of this event. Further details will be forwarded to you upon receipt of your written affirmative reply.

Sincerely,

William Denis Fugazy
Chairman

"Author's nomination for the Ellis Island
Medal of Honor Award, 1999."

"Author's patented antenna system used at the National Aerospace and Ionosphere Center in Arecibo, Puerto Rico."

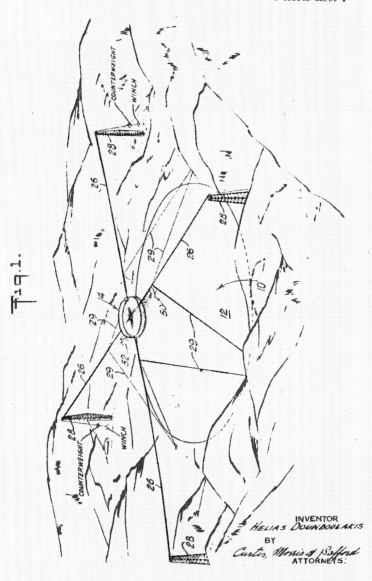

Fig.1.

The only one patent that exists on Arecibo Antenna was given to Helias Doundoulakis on Sept. 13, 1966, indicating the present Suspension System with cables and Towers.

Circled name of author on plaque left on the moon's surface by the Apollo 11 astronauts Neil Armstrong and Buzz Aldrin, 1969.

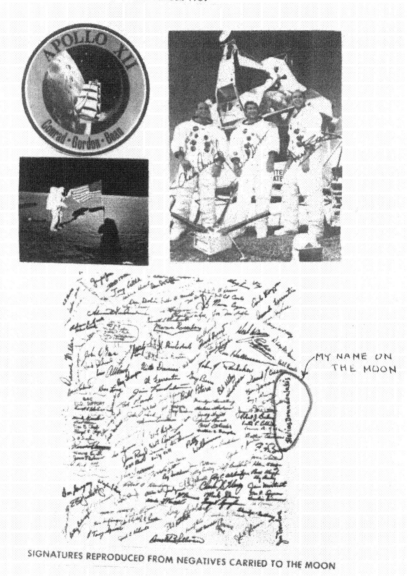

"Circled name of author on plaque left on the moon's surface
by the Apollo 12 astronauts, 1969."

Helias and Rita Doundoulakis

"Family Reunion, Christmas, 2005."